Quantitatives Controlling

Series editor
C. Homburg, Köln, Germany

The series serves as a panel for outstanding research in the field of accounting. The underlying concept of accounting goes beyond the scope of traditional corporate accounting including, for instance, aspects of behavior control. The series focuses on quantitative analyses of current topics in management and financial accounting and considers both analytical and empirical research designs.

Edited by
Univ.-Prof. Dr. Carsten Homburg
Universität zu Köln

More information about this series at http://www.springer.com/series/12419

Kristina Reimer

Asymmetric Cost Behavior

Implications for the Credit and Financial Risk of a Firm

With a foreword by Univ.-Prof. Dr. Carsten Homburg

Springer Gabler

Kristina Reimer
Köln, Germany

Dissertation Universität zu Köln 2017

Quantitatives Controlling
ISBN 978-3-658-22821-7 ISBN 978-3-658-22822-4 (eBook)
https://doi.org/10.1007/978-3-658-22822-4

Library of Congress Control Number: 2018948631

Springer Gabler

Printed on acid-free paper

This Springer Gabler imprint is published by the registered company Springer Fachmedien Wiesbaden GmbH part of Springer Nature
The registered company address is: Abraham-Lincoln-Str. 46, 65189 Wiesbaden, Germany

Geleitwort

Die vorliegende Dissertation beschäftigt sich mit dem Phänomen des asymmetrischen Kostenverhaltens (Kostenremanenz) und den Auswirkungen dieses Phänomens auf das Kredit- und Finanzrisiko eines Unternehmens. Die Arbeit ist in sechs Kapitel unterteilt. Nach der Einführung werden die theoretischen Grundlagen der Kostenremanenz sowie die Grundlagen des Kreditrisikos dargestellt. Die Arbeit beinhaltet weiterhin zwei empirische Studien, welche die Effekte der Kostenremanenz auf das Kredit- und Finanzrisiko untersuchen. In der Schlussbetrachtung werden die Einschränkungen der Dissertation diskutiert sowie Vorschläge für weitere Überlegungen herausgearbeitet.

Kapitel 1 befasst sich mit dem Konzept der Kostenremanenz. Beginnend mit den ersten Erwähnungen in den zwanziger Jahren des letzten Jahrhunderts wird die Literatur aufgearbeitet und die Ergebnisse des Forschungsstands präsentiert. Im nächsten Schritt werden die theoretischen Grundlagen analysiert. Zu diesem Zweck werden Ursprung, Entstehungsursachen und empirische Modelle erarbeitet, sowie das Konzept der Kostenremanenz kritisch betrachtet. Dabei werden die Ursachen umfassend und gründlich systematisch dargestellt und diskutiert.

Die Kategorisierung der Ursachen ist in diesem Umfang und Detailreichtum neu in der Forschungsliteratur. Insbesondere werden die Entstehungsursachen in Abhängigkeit von der Intention des Managements analysiert.

Weiterhin werden innerhalb der theoretischen Grundlagen der Arbeit die empirischen Modelle zur Messung der Kostenremanenz analysiert, verglichen und die Vor- und Nachteile diskutiert. Im zweiten Teil vom Kapitel 2 wird ein Literaturüberblick zum Thema asymmetrisches Kostenverhalten gegeben. Dabei werden die empirischen Studien gemäß ihrer primären Hauptziele kategorisiert: Nachweis der Existenz, Untersuchung der Determinanten sowie Implikationen der Kostenremanenz. Das Kapitel schließt mit einer kritischen Würdigung der Kostenasymmetrie.

In Antizipation der darauffolgenden empirischen Studie stellt das dritte Kapitel die theoretischen Grundlagen zum Thema Kreditrisiko dar. Nach der Definition und Klassifikation des Begriffs folgen Analyse und Vergleich der Modelle zur Messung des Kreditrisikos eines Unternehmens. Dabei wird neben den etablierten theoretischen Modellen wie Struktur- und Intensitätsmodelle das Kreditderivat

Credit Default Swap (CDS) zur Messung des Kreditrisikos anhand der Ergebnisse der aktuellen empirischen Studien untersucht und diskutiert.

Das vierte Kapitel umfasst eine empirische Studie, welche die Auswirkungen von Kostenremanenz auf das Kreditrisiko eines Unternehmens untersucht. Bei einem Umsatzrückgang werden Ressourcen freigesetzt. Unabhängig von der Quelle der Kostenremanenz, d.h. unabhängig davon, ob die Kostenremanenz das Resultat einer rationalen Handlung des Managements, eines Agency Problems oder als Konsequenz der in der Vergangenheit getroffenen Entscheidungen ist, wird die Kostenremanenz als Investition in ein riskantes Projekt angesehen, dessen Rendite von der unsicheren zukünftigen Nachfrage abhängt. Damit erhöht sich das Kreditrisiko, dass die Unternehmen ihren zukünftigen Zahlungsverpflichtungen nicht nachkommen können. Aufgrund der Ergebnisse der aktuellen Forschungsliteratur im relevanten Themengebiet werden insgesamt drei Wege ausgearbeitet, wie Kostenremanenz das Kreditrisiko beeinflusst.

Die durchgeführte Studie bereichert die Rechnungslegungs- sowie die Finanzliteratur. In Bezug auf die Rechnungslegungsliteratur wird eine neue Implikation der Kostenremanenz identifiziert und analysiert. Die Finanzliteratur wird durch die Dokumentation einer neuen Determinante in der Preisgestaltung der CDS Prämien bereichert. Das Ergebnis der negativen Kreditmarktreaktion auf das asymmetrische Kostenverhalten ist ebenfalls von praktischer Bedeutung. Manager können von der Erkenntnis profitieren, dass der Verzicht auf Ressourcenanpassungen bei einem Umsatzrückgang zum erhöhten Kreditrisiko und damit zu höheren Finanzierungskosten führt. Eine weitere praktische Konsequenz ist, dass die Erkenntnisse der Studie Gläubigern, Analysten und Ratingagenturen helfen können, das Kreditrisiko in Bezug auf asymmetrische Kostenentscheidungen genauer zu prognostizieren.

Das fünfte Kapitel umfasst eine weitere empirische Studie, welche den Einfluss des asymmetrischen Kostenverhaltens auf das finanzielle Risiko eines Unternehmens untersucht. Während in der ersten empirischen Studie der Fokus auf den Implikationen für die Fremdkapitalgeber liegt, analysiert die zweite Studie Auswirkungen der Kostenremanenz im Hinblick auf die Eigenkapitalgeber. Es wird eine Hypothese hergeleitet ausgehend vom Risiko über das Niveau und die Stabilität des operativen Cashflows eines Unternehmens mit ausgeprägter Kostenremanenz. Es wird argumentiert, dass die Eigentümer eine Kompensation für das zusätzliche Risiko verlangen, welches sich in erhöhten Prämien widerspiegelt.

In der Schlussbetrachtung der Dissertation werden die Einschränkungen der Studien besprochen sowie Vorschläge für weitere Forschung aufgeführt. Diese umfassen die Untersuchung des optimalen Grads an Kostenremanenz, die Unterscheidung zwischen der „guten“ (wertsteigender) und “schlechten“ (wertsenkender) Kostenremanenz, die Analyse der nicht intendierten und unvermeidbaren Kostenremanenz und schließlich das asymmetrische Kostenverhalten in Non-Profit-Organisationen.

Insgesamt ist der Autorin eine hervorragende Arbeit gelungen, die sich durch einen hohen Innovationsgrad auszeichnet.

Univ.-Prof. Dr. C. Homburg

Vorwort

Die vorliegende Arbeit entstand während meiner Tätigkeit als wissenschaftliche Mitarbeiterin am Seminar für Allgemeine Betriebswirtschaftslehre und Controlling der Universität zu Köln. Nach erfolgreichem Abschluss meiner Promotion möchte ich die folgenden Zeilen dazu nutzen, den Personen zu danken, die zum erfolgreichen Abschluss meines Dissertationsprojektes beigetragen haben.

Zuallererst möchte ich mich herzlich bei meinem Doktorvater und akademischen Lehrer, Herrn Prof. Dr. Carsten Homburg für die vielfältige Unterstützung sowie die Gewährung des zeitlichen und geistigen Freiraums bei der Erstellung dieser Arbeit bedanken. Unseren persönlichen und fachlichen Austausch habe ich sehr geschätzt. Mein weiterer Dank gilt Frau Prof. Uhrig-Homburg und Frau Jun.-Prof. Julia Nasev für die anregenden und sehr lehrreichen Diskussionen. Weiterhin danke ich dem Förderverein Controlling, dessen finanzielle Unterstützung die Teilnahme an internationalen wissenschaftlichen Konferenzen sowie die Beschaffung der für die Forschung notwendigen empirischen Daten ermöglicht hat. Ebenso möchte ich Herrn Prof. Dr. Thomas Hartmann-Wendels für die Übernahme des Zweitgutachtens und Herrn Prof. Dr. Ludwig Kuntz für den Vorsitz bei meiner Disputation danken.

Meinen Lehrstuhlkollegen Dr. Daniel Baumgarten, Dr. Max Berens, Dr. Snjezana Deno, Dr. Sebastian Gell, André Hoppe, Dr. Tanja Lorenz, Dr. Christian Müller-Hammerstein, Sabine Nentwig, Jun.-Prof. Julia Nasev, Dr. Dominik Nußman, Dr. Philipp Plank, Lars Rothe, Roman Schick, Dr. Simon Zehnder danke ich für die sehr gute Zusammenarbeit, die interessanten Diskussionen und die schöne gemeinsame Zeit. Ein besonderer Dank gilt meiner lieben Kollegin Dr. Stefanie Liesenfeld, die mir durch viele anregende Gespräche zu einer wertvollen und freundschaftlichen Wegbegleiterin wurde. Weiterer Dank gilt den studentischen Hilfskräften des Lehrstuhls, die mit ihrem Engagement wertvolle Hilfestellungen in Forschung und Lehre gaben. Weiterhin danke ich den ehemaligen Mitarbeitern des Seminars, insbesondere Prof. Dr. Sönke Sievers und Dr. Ute Bonenkamp für die einzigartige Hilfsbereitschaft und stets guten Rat. Nicht zuletzt möchte ich mich bei Elisabeth Tokarski-Eich und Tanja Breuer für die vielseitige Unterstützung bedanken. Ihre Erfahrung und Hilfsbereitschaft haben maßgeblich zu dem herzlichen und harmonischen Arbeitsklima am Lehrstuhl beigetragen.

Im privaten Bereich danke ich meinen Freundeskreis, der immer an mich geglaubt und unterstützt hat. Besonderer Dank gilt meinen Eltern Ludmilla und Waldemar Romaker, meiner Schwester Lena und meinen viel zu früh verstorbenen Großeltern. Mit ihrer bedingungslosen Unterstützung haben sie mir einen großen Rückhalt während meines Studiums und meiner Dissertation geboten.

Der allergrößte Dank gebührt meinem Ehemann Andreas und meiner Tochter Sophia. Eure Liebe, Geduld und Verständnis haben diese Arbeit möglich gemacht. In Liebe und Dankbarkeit ist dieses Buch Euch gewidmet.

Kristina Reimer

Table of Contents

List of Figures

List of Tables

List of Abbreviations

ABJ	Anderson, Banker, and Janakiraman
BIS	Bank for International Settlements
bn	billion
CDS	Credit Default Swap
CEO	Chief Executive Officer
COGS	Costs of Goods Sold
CRSP	Center for Research in Security Prices
e.g.	exempli gratia (for example)
Eq. (Eqs.)	Equation (Equations)
et al.	et alii (and others)
etc.	et cetera
EURO STOXX 50	Stock index of Eurozone stocks
exp.	expected
FE	Fixed Effects
GDP	Gross Domestic Product
i.e.	id est (that is)
ISDA	International Swaps and Derivatives Association
MM	Mille Mille (thousand thousands)
MV	Market Value
OLS	Ordinary Least Squares
OTC	Over-The-Counter
p.	page
p.a.	per annum
pp.	pages
R&D	Research and Development
RE	Random Effects
RTW	Right-to-Work
S&P 500	Standard & Poor's 500
s.d.	standard deviation
SEC	Securities and Exchange Commission
SG&A	Selling, General and Administrative
SIC	Standard Industrial Classification
UK	United Kingdom
US	United States

USA	United States of America
Vol.	Volume

List of Symbols

Latin Symbols

B	value of the default-risk-free bond
B^*	market value of a risky debt
B_0	price of defaultable bond matured in T
$BETA\_R_{i,t}$	proxy for CAPM beta of firm i at year t not explained by cost stickiness
$BETA_{i,t}$	CAPM beta of firm i at time t
$BM\_R_{i,t}$	proxy for book-to-market ratio of firm i at year t not explained by cost stickiness
$BM_{i,t}$	book-to-market ratio of firm i at year t
c	coupon payment
$COE_{i,t}$	expected cost of capital of firm i for year t
$COND_{i,t}$	proxy for favourable conditions of firm i at time t
$Control_{i,t}$	one of the control variables of firm i at year t
$Cost_{i,t\,(t-1)}$	costs of firm i in period end of t, $t-1$ respectively
cs	credit spread
$CUMR_{i,t}$	indicator variable equal to 1 if the CDS contract of firm i at time t has a full restructuring clause and 0 otherwise
D	face value of firm's debt
D_k	indicator variable denoting CDS maturities of k years
$D\_STICKY_{i,t}$	dummy variable equal to 1 if a firm i exhibits sticky cost behavior in period end of t and 0 otherwise
$Decrease\_Dummy_{i,t-1}$	indicator variable equal to 1 when activity level decreases from the period $t-1$ to t, and 0 otherwise
$EARNINGS_{i,t\,(t-1)}$	income before extraordinary items of firm i in period end of t, $t-1$ respectively
$EXR_{i,t}$	indicator variable equal to 1 if the CDS contract of firm i at time t has no restructuring clause and 0 otherwise

HML_m	value benchmark factor during month m
$\overline{HML}$	expected annual excess return on value portfolio
i	index for a stock or firm
L	leverage ratio
$L\_STICKY_{i,t}$	lag operator applied on $STICKY_{i,t+1}$
$LEV\_R_{i,t}$	proxy for leverage of firm i at year t not explained by cost stickiness
$LEV\_UA_{i,t}$	unadjusted leverage of firm i in period end of t computed as long term debt scaled by the value of assets
$LEV_{i,t}$	leverage of firm i in period end of t not explained by cost stickiness
$log(...)$	logarithm of (...)
$LOG\_CDS_{i,t(t+1)}$	natural logarithm of CDS spreads of firm i at quarter t, $t+1$ respectively
$LOGSIZE\_R_{i,t}$	proxy for size of firm i at year t not explained by cost stickiness
$LOGSIZE_{i,t}$	natural logarithm of the market value of firm i at year t
m	end of month m
$MV_{i,t}$	market value of equity of firm i at time t
N	number of observations
$N(.)$	standardized cumulative density function
P	value of the put option
q	survival probability
r^*	yield to maturity
R^2	coefficient of determination of regression
$REPUBLICAN_{i,t}$	indicator variable equal to 1, if firm i is headquartered in a state under influence of Republican Party at time t and 0 otherwise
r_f	risk-free interest rate
$\overline{r^f}$	expected annual risk-free rate
r_T^d	yield to maturity of a defaultable bond
r_T^f	yield to maturity of a default-risk-free bond
RF_t	risk-free rate at time t
$RMRF_m$	market benchmark factor during month m
$\overline{RMRF}$	expected annual excess return on market portfolio
$ROA\_R_{i,t}$	proxy for profitability of firm i at year t not

	explained by cost stickiness
$ROA\_UA_{i,t}$	unadjusted return on assets of a firm i at time t calculated as quarterly income before extraordinary items scaled by total assets in the previous period
$ROA_{i,t}$	return on assets of a firm i at time t not explained by cost stickiness
$RTW_{i,t}$	indicator variable equal to 1 if a firm i is headquartered in a state that passed right-to-work law up to time t
$SENIORITY_{i,t}$	indicator variable equal to 1 if the underlying CDS contract of firm i at time t is senior and 0 otherwise
$SG\&A_{i,t\ (t-1)}$	Selling, general and administrative costs of firm i in period end of t, $t-1$ respectively
$SIZE\_UA_{i,t}$	unadjusted firm size of firm i in period end of t computed as logarithm of market value
$SIZE_{i,t}$	size of firm i in period end of t not explained by cost stickiness
SMB	size benchmark factor during month m
$\overline{SMB}$	expected annual return on size portfolio
$SPREAD_{i,t}$	CDS spread in basis points of CDS contract of firm i at time t
$STICKY_{i,t}$	measure for the stickiness of a firm i at time t
t	period t, proxy for different time variables
T	maturity date of a debt
$VOL\_UA_{i,t}$	standard deviation of daily returns of firm i during the firm's current fiscal quarter
$VOL_{i,t}$	proxy for asset volatility of firm i of firm i not explained by cost stickiness
V_t	asset value of a firm at time t
V_T	asset value of a firm at time T

Greek Symbols

α	regression coefficient or intercept
β	regression coefficient or intercept
$\hat{\beta}$	estimated value of regression coefficient or intercept
β^l	loading on factor l
δ	coefficient indicating the first derivative
$\Delta COST$	change in costs
$\Delta SALE$	change in sales
ε	error term, residual of a regression
γ	recovery rate
$\overline{\tau}$	most recent of the last four quarters (years) with an increase in sales
$\underline{\tau}$	most recent of the last four quarters (years) with a decrease in sales
σ	standard deviation of returns on the asset value

Further Symbols

$	Dollar
*** (**, *)	significance at the 1 %- (5 %-, 10 %) level
ATQ	total assets at quarter end
CEQ	common equity
CSHOQ	common shares outstanding
DLTTQ	long term debt at quarter end
IBQ	quarterly income before extraordinary items
LTQ	total liabilities at quarter end
PRCCQ	close price at quarter end
RET	daily return
SALEQ	sales at quarter end

1 Introduction

Understanding cost behavior is crucial for various participants of capital markets. Managers for example are engaged to manage costs efficiently since costs determine earnings, which in turn are often used to evaluate firms' and managers' performance. More specifically, in competitive markets where the prices are predetermined, managers can increase profitability by focusing on costs. Analysts, creditors, and investors for example make significant efforts to analyze and predict cost behavior since it is highly relevant in line with predicting sales in order to estimate future earnings more precisely. Further, corporate outsiders evaluate firms' performance inter alia on management's ability to efficiently control costs.

The traditional view of cost behavior distinguishes between fixed and variable costs with regard to changes in the activity level of a firm. Fixed costs are considered to be independent of the activity level,[1] where variable costs are assumed to be proportional with respect to the changes in the activity level (Noreen 1991). However, contrary to this traditional view of linear and proportional cost behavior, various studies find empirical evidence for asymmetric cost behavior. This new era of asymmetric cost behavior in the accounting literature was initiated by Anderson, Banker, and Janakiraman (2003) who documented that the relation of cost and volume depends on direction of activity changes and that costs decrease less when activity level decreases than they increase for an equivalent activity increase. Costs exhibiting the described asymmetric behavior are labeled as "sticky" and the phenomenon of asymmetric cost behavior as "cost stickiness". A large number of subsequent studies have examined the sources, determinants, and consequences of the asymmetric cost behavior. The main objective of my doctoral thesis is thus to deliver a comprehensive literature overview of the existing theoretical and empirical findings in this area and to provide empirical evidence of two new implications of asymmetric cost behavior.

For this purpose I first present the cost stickiness concept as a whole in Chapter 2. Thereby I analyze and structure the most important findings in the asymmetric cost behavior literature. I start with the origin of asymmetric cost behavior in the research literature and continue with a theoretical discussion of various sources for the cost stickiness occurrence. In the second part of Chapter 2 I provide a

---

[1] More precisely, fixed costs are independent from the changes in activity level only in the short run since in the long run all costs are variable (see Cooper and Kaplan 1988, p. 27).

K. Reimer, *Asymmetric Cost Behavior*, Quantitatives Controlling,
https://doi.org/10.1007/978-3-658-22822-4_1

comprehensive literature review of the most important empirical research papers on asymmetric costs in the accounting research and assign them to models, empirical evidence on the existence of cost stickiness, its determinants, and implications. I further discuss the contrarian claims against asymmetric cost behavior and review research studies that criticize the cost stickiness concept. Thus, Chapter 2 builds a theoretical fundament for my doctoral thesis and offers a comprehensive and structured review of the cost stickiness literature.

Chapter 3 provides a basic framework of credit risk fundamentals required for the empirical study in Chapter 4. I first review the main theoretical models, structural and reduced-form models for pricing credit risk. A considerable part of this chapter is dedicated to the most popular credit derivative, namely the credit default swap (CDS). Since its creation by J.P. Morgan in 1994, the CDS market has experienced enormous growth. Although the CDS market has been subject to considerable decline since the financial crisis of 2008, it still remains a highly sizable and important part of credit derivative market. I provide an overview of the CDS market development in detail and discuss the underlying reasons for its fluctuation. Moreover, CDSs are popular instruments for researchers measuring credit risk in empirical analyses since they are considered to be a pure measure of credit risk. I therefore discuss and review in detail the research studies that provide evidence of the superiority of CDSs compared to other instruments before closing the chapter with a discussion on the applicability of CDSs in measuring credit risk in general.

As I will show in my thesis, huge efforts have been made towards understanding the determinants and sources for asymmetric cost behavior over the last two decades. Yet rather than focusing on understanding what determines this phenomenon, I center my research on providing new insights into the consequences of cost stickiness. The necessity of furnishing management and corporate insiders with practical advice has been underlined more than once in leading accounting journals. For example, in her editorial "Management Accountant—What Ails Thee?", Ranjani Krishnan, the editor in chief at the Journal of Management Accounting Research (2012-2015), called upon academics to conduct research that carries the potential to be applied in practice (Krishnan 2015). Following this advice I examine the impact of asymmetric cost behavior on credit risk in Chapter 4 of my doctoral thesis. More precisely, I document strong evidence for an impact of cost behavior on credit risk. After controlling for well-known credit risk determinants I find that cost stickiness is positively and significantly related to firm credit risk. In particular, one standard deviation increase in cost stickiness leads to a 27 basis points increase in CDS spreads on average. The findings hold for CDSs on both senior and subordinated debt of all maturities and are robust to different lag structures, variable measurement, and alternative model specifications. Overall, the findings are consistent with a structural credit model perspective: More stickiness leads to higher earnings volatility and higher accounting information risk, which increases the firm's default probability and credit risk.

Another contribution of my doctoral thesis is that I provide strong empirical evidence on the relevance of cost stickiness for influencing financial risk of equity. The riskiness of future cash flows arising from sticky costs results in a higher expected risk premium of the equity holders. As predicted, I document that cost stickiness increases the expected cost of equity measured by the Fama French Three Factor Model. The results suggest that cost stickiness and fundamental characteristics are correlated and reflect some common but also incremental information about the cost of equity to that captured by fundamentals. The described empirical study is presented in Chapter 5 of the thesis.

The empirical findings of my doctoral thesis are useful for management, firm owners, creditors, analysts, as well as researchers. Management may benefit from the awareness that maintaining redundant resources results in higher credit and financial risk and thus, higher cost of capital. Creditors and firm owners can better assess the risk of their investments in firms exhibiting sticky cost behavior. Analysts and credit rating agencies may benefit from my findings in better predicting credit and financial risk associated with cost stickiness. Further, my findings also contribute to the accounting and finance literature. With regard to accounting literature, I extend the prior work on asymmetric cost behavior by providing new implication of cost stickiness. With respect to finance literature, my results contribute to credit derivative and cost of equity literature by documenting that cost behavior plays a significant role in the pricing of credit derivatives as well as equity risk.

Finally, I summarize and discuss the limitations of my results before providing suggestions for further research in Chapter 6. Figure 1.1 illustrates the structure of the thesis.

Figure 1.1: Structure of the Thesis

Chapter 2	Structured literature review of cost stickiness concept
Chapter 3	Theoretical framework of credit risk fundamentals
Chapter 4	Empirical study: Implications of cost stickiness on credit risk
Chapter 5	Empirical Study: Implications of cost stickiness on financial risk
Chapter 6	Summary and suggestions for future research

2 Cost Stickiness Concept

This chapter provides the framework for the two empirical studies presented in the subsequent chapters of my thesis. Section 2.1 describes the origin and development of the cost stickiness concept in the research literature. Section 2.2 considers various sources for cost stickiness occurrence and classifies them. Section 2.3 introduces the empirical models of asymmetric cost behavior. Section 2.4 presents research studies of cost stickiness categorizing them into existence, determinants, and the implications of cost stickiness. Section 2.5 addresses the contradicting claims made against the cost stickiness concept in the accounting literature.

K. Reimer, *Asymmetric Cost Behavior*, Quantitatives Controlling,
https://doi.org/10.1007/978-3-658-22822-4_2

Figure 2.1: Structure of Chapter 2

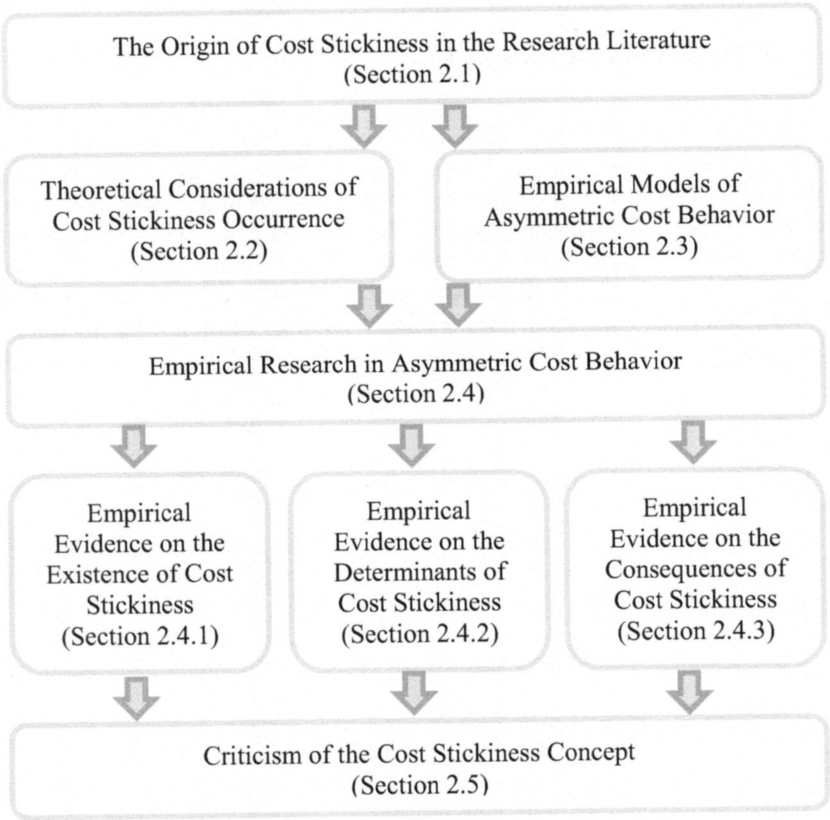

2.1 The Origin of Cost Stickiness in the Research Literature

The traditional models of cost behavior, established in the accounting literature, differentiate between *fixed* and *variable* costs[2] with respect to changes in activity volume.[3] These models assume proportional change of variable costs with changes in the activity level (Noreen 1991). The assumption of proportionality is stronger than that of linearity, since it requires that a percentage change in activity level equals the percentage change of associated costs.[4] The conventional view of cost accounting implies that the level of a change in costs is independent of the direction of the activity change (decrease or increase).[5]

Several studies question proportional cost behavior both during the 20th century and afterwards. Already in the 1920s, the traditional view of linear or proportional cost behavior was challenged in the German research literature. Hasenack (1925) considers labor costs in the banking sector and rejects proportional cost behavior, pointing to slowness in the adjustment of labor costs during a recession. Hasenack (1925) designates proportional costs in the banking sector to be inefficient as a result of the costs associated with the firing and hiring of employees.[6] Assuming the efficiency at the level of maximum employment only, Hasenack (1925) postulates asymmetric adaptability of costs with regard to changing employment intensity.[7]

In a follow-up study, Brasch (1927) analyses changes in costs with regard to increasing and decreasing employment and ascertains an empirical inequality of the cost behavior conditional on the direction of employment's changes.[8] Motivated by the analogy to the remanent magnetization in response to decreasing magnetic field intensity, a regularity from electrophysics, Brasch (1927) introduces the term "*Remanenz der Unkosten*" ["*remanence of expenses*"].[9]

Strube (1936) investigates empirically the cost behavior of several companies, explicitly focusing on the phenomenon of asymmetric cost behavior, thereby finally

---

2 The differentiation between fixed and variable costs is a short-run notion, since in the long run all costs are variable within the meaning that all costs can be adjusted in the long run (see Cooper and Kaplan 1988, p. 27).

3 See Garrison, Noreen, and Brewer (2015) or Horngren, Datar, and Rajan (2015) for an accounting textbook example and Balakrishnan, Labro, and Soderstrom (2014), p. 92 or Banker and Byzalov (2014), pp. 43-44 for research studies.

4 See e.g., Noreen and Soderstrom (1994), p. 256.

5 See Anderson, Banker, and Janakiraman (2003), p. 48.

6 See Hasenack (1925), p. 83.

7 See Hasenack (1925), p. 91.

8 See Brasch (1927), p. 67.

9 Brasch (1927), p. 68.

anchoring the term *cost remanence* in the research literature.[10] In addition, Strube (1936) provides a range of sources of asymmetric cost behavior.[11]

From the 1990s onwards empirical research has continued to question proportional cost behavior, showing the link between direction of the change in activity level and the magnitude of the changes in costs. Noreen and Soderstrom (1994) test empirically the proportional cost model by analyzing the overhead costs. Using data from hospitals in Washington State, the authors reject the proportional hypothesis by detecting decline in average costs in response to an increase in activity level in most overhead accounts.[12]

In a subsequent study, Noreen and Soderstrom (1997) focus on the time-series behavior of costs. By examining overhead costs from 108 hospitals from 1977 through 1992, the authors document that only 20% of overhead costs variate with the activity driver.[13] Noreen and Soderstrom (1997) conclude that any cost model assuming proportional cost behavior will overstate the marginal costs and that even strict fixed cost models will provide more accurate costs' forecasts.[14] In addition, Noreen and Soderstrom (1997) report modest evidence for asymmetric cost behavior: costs decrease less when the activity level decreases than they increase in response to increasing activity in 3 of 16 cost accounts.[15]

In their influential study, Anderson, Banker, and Janakiraman (2003) build on the results of Noreen and Soderstrom (1994, 1997) and empirically address the question of whether the relation of cost and volume depends on the direction of activity changes. Based on the data from 1,817 US firms over the sample period from 1979 through 1998, Anderson, Banker, and Janakiraman (2003) document that selling, general and administrative (SG&A) costs increase on average 0.55% per 1%

---

10 The terms cost remanence and cost stickiness are treated as synonyms in the past decades (see Guenther, Riehl, and Rößler 2014 for an example). Originally, the term cost remanence signified the remanent costs, i.e., staying behind the changes in activity level, implying in addition the remanence of costs by an activity level increase (see Malagoli 1985, p. 54). In my dissertation thesis I apply the definition from Anderson, Banker, and Janakiraman (2003), considering only the remanence of costs by an activity level decrease, the modern definition from the Anglo-American literature.

11 See Strube (1936), pp. 19-21.

12 The proportional costs model implies constant average costs, thus, a decrease in average costs indicates non-proportional cost behavior.

13 In a two-period form of regression model, Noreen and Soderstrom (1997) find that 33% of all costs are proportional (see Noreen and Soderstrom 1997, Table 6, p. 104 and Table 7, p. 105 for the results based on one-period and two-period form of regression model respectively).

14 When the costs are strictly proportional, the marginal costs are equal to average costs, where non-proportional cost behavior results in higher average costs compared to marginal costs. This assumes that proportional costs result in an overstatement of marginal costs.

15 See Noreen and Soderstrom (1997), Table 9, p. 107.

increase in revenue, while they decrease only 0.35% per 1% decrease in revenue. Thereby, the authors define ultimately the costs that decrease less for activity decreases as they increase for an equivalent activity increase as *sticky costs* and the described phenomenon as *asymmetric cost behavior* or *cost stickiness*.

2.2 Theoretical Considerations of Cost Stickiness Occurrence

The sources of cost stickiness are manifold and variable in their nature. Based on the results of Anderson, Banker, and Janakiraman (2003), much of the literature focuses on the economic and agency drivers of cost stickiness and, more recently, behavioral sources. The aim of this section is to provide a comprehensive overview of the potential drivers of asymmetric cost behavior. For this purpose I differentiate between cost stickiness resulting from deliberating management decisions, and thus intended by a firm's management, which is presented in Section 2.2.1, and unintended resulting from other reasons, which I consider in Section 2.2.2.[16] Figure 2.2 illustrates this differentiation.

Figure 2.2: Cost Stickiness Sources

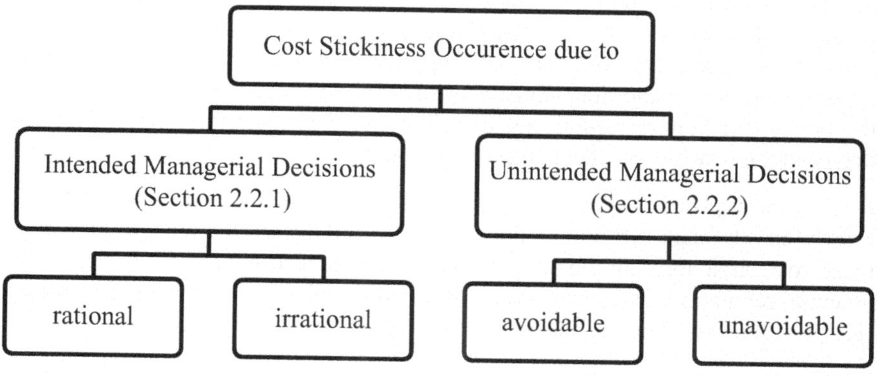

2.2.1 Sources for Intended Cost Stickiness

As shown in Figure 2.2, cost stickiness may occur from the intended managerial decisions, which can be further classified as rational or irrational. I designate

16 An early example of differentiating between intended and unintended sources of sticky costs can be found in Malagoli (1985).

managerial choice as rational when management operates in the interests of a firm (or organization),[17] i.e., rational from the firm's perspective, and irrational otherwise.

2.2.1.1 *Rational Managerial Decisions*

In their seminal paper Anderson, Banker, and Janakiraman (2003) provide the most intuitive explanation for asymmetric cost behavior, namely: asymmetric frictions in resource adjustments. That is, the upward adjustment is less constrained than the downward adjustment with regard to demand changes (e.g., Jaramillo, Schiantarelli, and Sembenelli 1993; Goux, Maurin, and Pauchet 2001; Cooper and Haltiwanger 2006). The presence of costs arising from the adjustment of resources in response to the activity level decrease lead the managers to a trade-off decision between the costs resulting from maintenance redundant resources and from resource adjustment. When the demand falls and managers renounce the adjustment of resources, the capacity releases and holding costs of unused capacity occur such as wages or depreciation. On the other hand, if management decides to cut the redundant resources, adjustment costs arise. Adjustment costs include, inter alia, severance payments, costs caused by premature cancellations of contracts, and costs of disposal. Further, subsequent costs occur in the future through the adjustment to the high activity level, e.g., search and hiring costs of new employees, transaction costs of new contract negotiations with suppliers, and installation and customizing costs of facilities. In addition, adjustment costs involve organizational costs such as the erosion of human capital and therefore lower productivity caused through decreasing motivation or the disruption of teams.[18]

Besides the adjustment costs incurred immediately in the firm, the loss of a firm's reputation, although difficult to quantify, falls within the adjustment costs since these costs arise through the adjustment of redundant resources. More precisely, potential reputation losses negatively affect future sales and a firm's performance (Karpoff, Lee, and Martin 2008) and thus represent opportunity costs.

Further, since demand is uncertain, management must evaluate the likelihood as to whether a decrease in demand is temporary and take this into consideration. Cost stickiness arises when the assessed present value of adjustment costs prevails over the present value of holding costs as a consequence of rational management acting.

---

17 For simplicity, I assume at this point 100% equity financing due to divergence in objectives of equity and debt holders. For example, debt holders would prefer less risky and less profitable investments since they only receive a fixed portion of generated income, while equity holders benefit from high cash flow.

18 See Anderson, Banker, and Janakiraman (2003), p. 49.

Various studies confirm the adjustment cost explanation of sticky costs by providing empirical tests with evidence of the relation between the level of adjustment costs and the level of cost stickiness by using different empirical adjustment proxies. For example, Anderson, Banker, and Janakiraman (2003) show that higher employee and asset intensity increase cost stickiness. Using hospital data, Balakrishnan and Gruca (2008) document higher cost stickiness in the patient services compared to support services due to higher adjustment costs in the core activity. Banker, Byzalov, and Chen (2013) use employment protection legislation provisions in different countries as a proxy for labor adjustment costs and document statistically and economically significant association between cost stickiness at the firm level and the strictness of employment protection legislation.

To summarize, cost stickiness caused by adjustment costs is a result of a rational deliberate management decision aimed to maximize firm value in the long run and therefore falls into category of economic sources (Figure 2.3).

Figure 2.3: The Dimensions of Rational Managerial Decisions

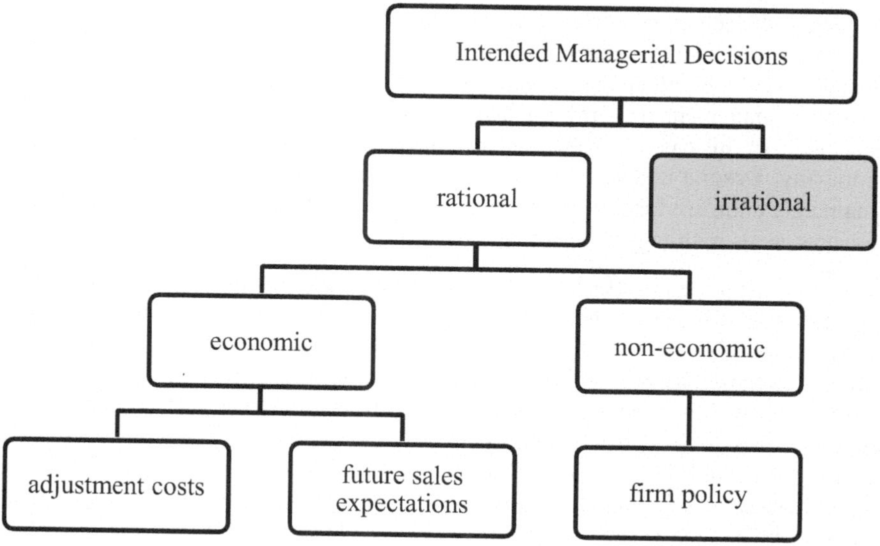

Another source of cost stickiness is *managers' sales expectations in the future*. When managers have primarily positive future sales expectations, they are less inclined to cut redundant resources during a current sales decrease due to their planned use in the near future. Likewise, in the case of a current sales increase managers will be more willing to increase capacity since the demand reverse is unlikely.[19] Thus, positive demand expectations increase cost stickiness even if adjustment costs are symmetric.[20]

Empirical tests for the managerial expectations for future sales, as one of the cost stickiness' sources, are performed, for example, by Anderson, Banker, and Janakiraman (2003) as well as Banker, Byzalov, Ciftci, and Mashruwala (2014). Anderson, Banker, and Janakiraman (2003) use revenue decline in preceding period and gross domestic product (GDP) growth as a proxy for managerial optimism. As expected, they confirm the influence of managers' expectations for future sales on the degree of cost stickiness. Although Banker et al. (2014) do not find statistical significance for the role of GDP growth after controlling for order backlog, they document the relevance of managerial expectations using other proxies such as: two successive sales increases, analysts' sales forecasts and order backlog conditional on a prior sales increase.[21] In sum then, the presented empirical evidence reflects deliberately rational, economically motivated, managerial decisions causing cost stickiness.[22]

While the adjustment cost explanation and economic outlook result from rational managerial decisions and are economically motivated, other rational, but non-economic reasoned explanation, is conceivable. Companies themselves may pursue social objectives rather than primarily maximizing firm value. Due to the firm policy management may refrain from dismissals in periods marked by a sales decline.[23] In this case, management still operates rationally, i.e., in the interest of company. Despite underemployment, caused by demand decrease, management maintains unutilized resources even if the downward adjustment would be more advantageous with regard to firm value maximization.

Guenther, Riehl, and Rößler (2014) consider inter alia maintenance of unutilized resources as a result of the social conditions and expectations of a company's environment. The authors highlight that it is difficult to differentiate between cost stickiness caused by economic considerations and cost stickiness arising from social responsibility. Since the reputation losses negatively influence sales, reluctance to adjust resources by activity level decline may be economically reasoned and therefore should be considered as part of adjustment costs. Nevertheless, asymmetric cost behavior due to firm policy is possible simply due to the nature of organizations such as non-profit universities or hospitals. Finding evidence for sticky cost behavior in the patient services of hospitals, Balakrishnan and Gruca

19 See Banker and Byzalov (2014), p. 45.

20 See Banker, Byzalov, and Plehn-Dujowich (2011), p. 3.

21 See Banker et al. (2014), pp. 235-240.

22 I consider irrational sources of asymmetric cost behavior in Section 2.2.1.2 below.

23 See Strube (1936), p. 19.

(2008) attribute their result to higher adjustment costs but also to the responsibility of hospitals to guarantee qualitative patient care.[24]

2.2.1.2 Irrational Managerial Decisions

As already explained in Section 2.2.1, differentiating into rational and irrational acting is based on a firm's perspective. The categories of cost stickiness occurrence that arise from irrational management's operations are presented in Figure 2.4.

Figure 2.4: The Dimensions of Irrational Managerial Decisions

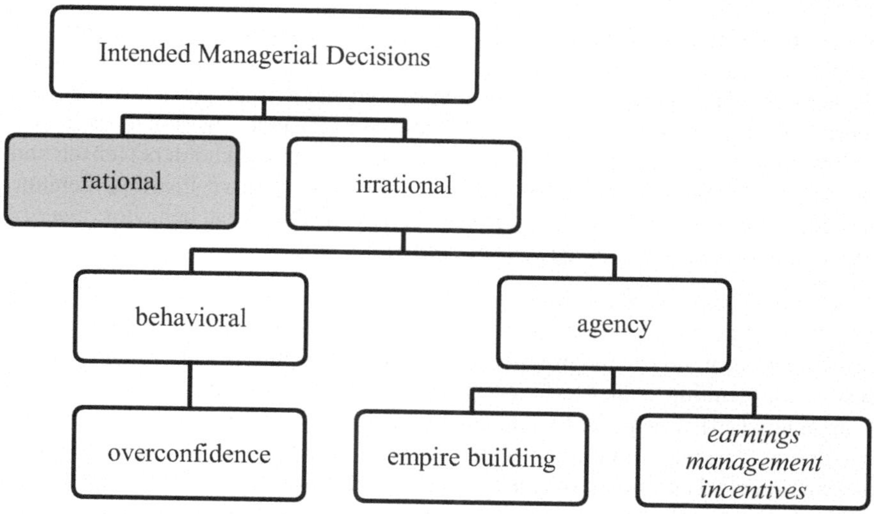

According to the behavioral explanation for cost stickiness, the overconfidence of managers increases cost stickiness. Overconfident managers tend to overestimate future sales and therefore do not adjust redundant resources in response to a sales decrease at the economically reasonable level. This results in a higher degree of cost stickiness.[25] Chen, Gores, and Nasev (2013) argue that overconfident managers will overestimate their ability to influence future sales as well as the accuracy of their assessment of future demand, resulting in an overestimation of future sales. Based on the psychological findings showing that individuals tend to be overconfident, Chen, Gores, and Nasev (2013) hypothesize that managerial overconfidence increases the degree of cost stickiness. Using chief executive officer (CEO)s' option

24 See Balakrishnan and Gruca (2008), p. 993.
25 See Chen, Gores, and Nasev (2013), pp. 3-4.

exercise behavior as a proxy for managerial overconfidence, as expected they find a positive association between overconfidence and cost stickiness after controlling for economic and agency factors.[26]

In additional tests Chen, Gores, and Nasev (2013) empirically distinguish between the overconfidence explanation and managerial rational expectation of future sales based on prior sales signals (Banker et al. 2014), documenting the incremental influence of managerial overconfidence beyond rational expectations of management. In a related paper, Qin, Mohan, and Kuang (2015) confirm the behavioral explanation of cost stickiness occurrence using the prominence of CEO's photography in an annual report as a proxy for overconfidence.

While the behavior explanation of asymmetric cost behavior can be accounted for the failure of management, according to agency explanation cost stickiness arises through the operations of quite able and competent managers, but who are motivated by their own interests. Self-interested managers maximize their own utility even if their actions diverge from the interests of stockholders (Jensen and Meckling 1976) and thus are irrational from a firm's perspective. Previous literature has identified two main agency drivers of asymmetric cost behavior: *empire building* and *earnings management incentives*.

Empire building describes an agency problem of managerial activities aimed to benefit from the firm's size (Jensen 1986). Due to the fear of losing prestige, power or compensation managers grow the firm beyond its optimal size or retain excess resources, resulting in an inefficient high level of cost stickiness. Chen, Lu, and Sougiannis (2012) empirically address this question and document that the cost asymmetry increases with managers' empire building incentives[27] and this association weakens with stronger corporate governance (e.g., with the number of institutional shareholders, a smaller board size or percentage of independent directors).[28]

However, earnings management incentives may result in an inefficient low level of cost stickiness.[29] Based on prior findings showing that agency considerations force managers to reduce costs to meet earnings targets, Kama and Weiss (2013) argue that self-interested (i.e., maximizing their own utility rather than firm value) managers will cut redundant resources, even if they assess demand decrease as

26 For details see Chen, Gores, and Nasev (2013), p 13.

27 Chen, Lu, and Sougiannis (2012) use four different proxies for managers' empire building incentives: free cash flow, the number of years a manager expects to remain in his position, CEO tenure, and CEO compensation (see Chen, Lu, and Sougiannis 2012, pp. 256-258).

28 For details see Chen, Lu, and Sougiannis (2012), pp. 261-262.

29 See Banker and Byzalov (2014), p. 53.

temporary and the downward resource adjustment is not optimal from the perspective of maximizing firm value.

Empirical evidence, confirming the hypothesis of the negative association between earnings management incentives to meet earnings targets and the level of cost stickiness, is provided by Dierynck, Landsman, and Renders (2012) in Belgian private companies, and by Kama and Weiss (2013) using the data of US firms.

2.2.2 Sources for Unintended Cost Stickiness

In contrast to the intended current deliberate managerial decisions to maintain unutilized resources by an activity level decrease, cost stickiness may occur as a result of previous managerial actions or under other conditions that cannot be influenced by management. Figure 2.5 illustrates this scenario.

Figure 2.5: Dimensions of Unintended Cost Stickiness

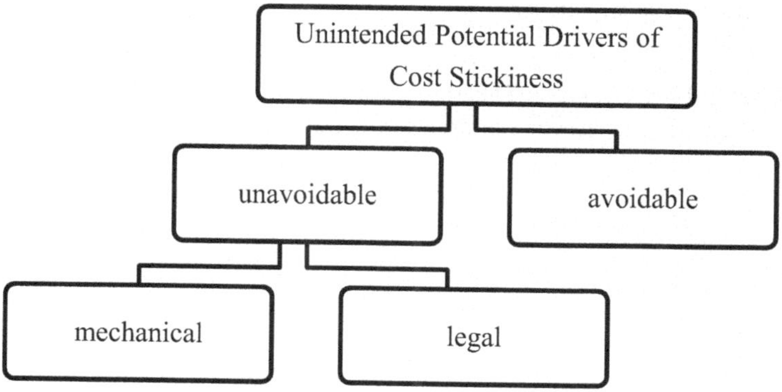

Anderson and Lanen (2009) criticize Anderson, Banker, and Janakiraman (2003) for interpreting the existence of asymmetric costs as "*evidence of active cost management*".[30] Thus past managerial decisions, even those such as the choice of technical or engineering production specifications may result in sticky cost behavior due to "*mechanistic*" changes in costs.[31] Kama and Weiss (2010) confirm empirically that the technological constraints imposed by previous technology choices result in a higher degree of cost stickiness.

30 Anderson and Lanen (2009), p. 3.
31 See Anderson and Lanen (2009), p. 3.

Without conducting empirical tests, Mahlendorf (2009) names contracts with fixed maturity which cannot be adjusted according to the activity changes, as examples of unavoidable cost stickiness.[32] Similarly, Guenther, Riehl, and Rößler (2014) theoretically consider legal reasons for unintended and unavoidable cost stickiness occurrence. The authors argue that requirements of employment and social legislation for dismissal rule out the adjustment of costs immediately in the period of sales decline. In addition, other institutions such as the supervisory board or works council may restrict management in cutting excess resources.[33] Thus, the legal constrains result in unavoidable and unintended cost stickiness. These legal limits differ considerably from those legal conditions such as bargaining power or high dismissal protection. While the latter may aggravate, they nevertheless allow cost adjustment and thus need to be considered as part of adjustment costs discussed in Section 2.2.1.

Lastly, asymmetric cost behavior may occur as a result of cognitive limitations, which are neither intended nor unavoidable. For instance, a failure by the accounting department to identify potential cost adjustment quickly and precisely may also cause cost stickiness.[34]

Figure 2.6 summarizes the previously discussed sources for intended (Section 2.2.1) and unintended cost stickiness (Section 2.2.2). In this context it should be noted that the presented drivers can be incomplete and can appear in conjunction with each other.

32 See Mahlendorf (2009), p. 193.
33 See Guenther, Riehl, and Rößler (2014), p. 303.
34 See Mahlendorf (2009), pp. 193-194.

Figure 2.6: Dimensions of Cost Stickiness[35]

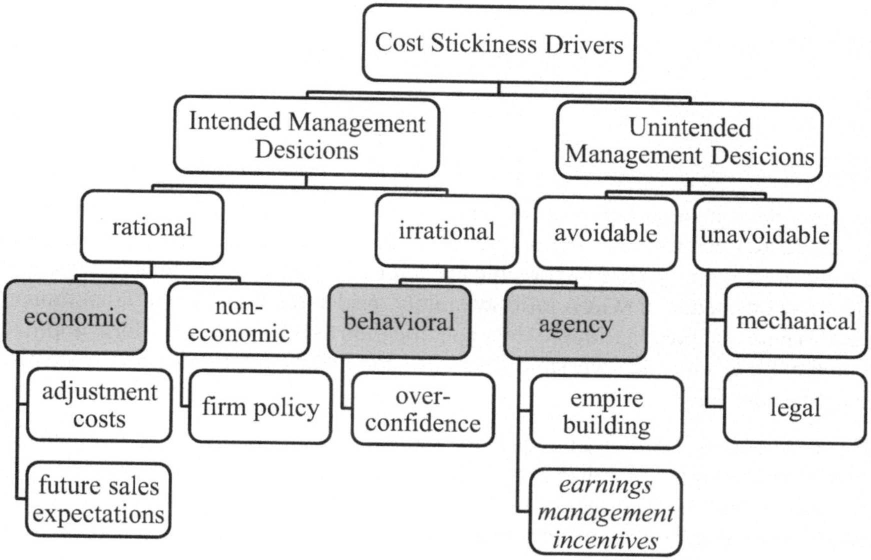

2.3 Empirical Models of Asymmetric Cost Behavior

2.3.1 The Model of Anderson, Banker, and Janakiraman (2003)

Anderson, Banker, and Janakiraman (2003) introduce the term cost stickiness and provide an empirical estimation model (ABJ Model) that allows for the testing of asymmetric cost behavior. More specifically, the model refers changes in SG&A costs to simultaneous changes in net sales revenue. The dependent variable is the logarithmic ratio of current SG&A to SG&A costs from the previous period; the independent variable is the logarithmic ratio of current to the preceding revenue:[36]

---

35 The gray shaded fields highlight the most commonly analyzed and discussed drivers for cost stickiness occurrence in empirical accounting research.

36 Anderson, Banker, and Janakiraman (2003) use sales revenue as an imperfect proxy for sales volume (i.e., physical quantity of items) since the physical output data is not directly observable.

$$log\left[\frac{SG\&A_{i,t}}{SG\&A_{i,t-1}}\right] = \beta_0 + \beta_1 \cdot log\left[\frac{Sales_{i,t}}{Sales_{i,t-1}}\right] + \beta_2 \cdot Decrease\_Dummy_{i,t} \cdot log\left[\frac{Sales_{i,t}}{Sales_{i,t-1}}\right] + \varepsilon_{i,t}. \quad 2.1$$

The interaction variable *Decrease_Dummy*$_{i,t}$ takes the value of 1 when the activity level decreases from the period *t-1* to *t*, and 0 otherwise. Thus, the variable *Decrease_Dummy*$_{i,t}$ makes it possible to capture the impact of revenue increase and decrease on change in SG&A ratio separately. Anderson, Banker, and Janakiraman (2003) note that the logarithmic (log) specification as well as the ratio form improve comparability of the variables across companies and mitigate potential heteroscedasticity.[37]

Since *Decrease_Dummy*$_{i,t}$ is equal to 0 when sales increase, the coefficient β_1 measures the percentage change in SG&A costs arising from a 1% increase in sales revenue, while the sum of β_1 and β_2 determines the percentage change in SG&A costs with a 1% decrease in sales revenue and β_2 represents the averaged degree of cost stickiness. The evidence of cost stickiness is given when the change in SG&A costs with revenue increase (β_1) is greater than the change for revenue decreases ($\beta_1 + \beta_2$). Empirically: the value of β_2 is significantly negative, given a positive value for β_1.

Although Anderson, Banker, and Janakiraman (2003) measure the stickiness of SG&A costs, their model can be applied to examine different components of SG&A or other types of costs. Various follow-up studies have modified the model of Anderson, Banker, and Janakiraman (2003) by introducing additional determinants of cost stickiness and/or studying different types of costs.[38]

In this manner, Banker and Byzalov (2014) provide a formula of a generalized ABJ model, which enables the consideration of additional determinants of sticky costs:

$$log\left[\frac{Cost_{i,t}}{Cost_{i,t-1}}\right] = \beta_0 + \delta_0^X X_{i,t} \quad 2.2$$

37 Heteroscedasticity refers to the differences in variance of error terms in the regression analysis and leads to, although unbiased, nevertheless inefficient ordinary least squares coefficient estimates, which result in biased standard errors and thus inappropriate confidence intervals (see Wooldridge 2013, p. 140).

38 I consider the stickiness of various cost components in Section 2.4.1.1.

$$+(\beta_1 + \delta_1^X X_{i,t}) \, log\left[\frac{Sales_{i,t}}{Sales_{i,t-1}}\right]$$

$$+(\beta_2 + \delta_2^X X_{i,t}) \cdot Decrease\_Dummy_{i,t}$$

$$\cdot \, log\left[\frac{Sales_{i,t}}{Sales_{i,t-1}}\right] + \varepsilon_{i,t},$$

where $X_{i,t}$ stands for a vector of observable determinants (e.g., asset intensity, GDP growth, etc.) of asymmetric cost behavior. The term $\delta_0^X X_{i,t}$ represents the stand alone effects of determinants on cost changes. The coefficient δ_1^X unequal to zero signals varying slope for sales increases with determinants of cost stickiness ($X_{i,t}$). In contrast, Anderson, Banker, and Janakiraman (2003) assume a mechanistic resource expansion in case of sales increases and therefore do not include determinants of cost asymmetry in the slope for sales increases.[39] Thus, the generalized formula of Banker and Byzalov (2014) further allows for the incorporation of managerial exercise discretion by adding the resources.

Although the evidence of cost stickiness is not dependent on the log specification, a linear model specification may be advantageous.[40] For example, the linear model specification may be preferred when analyzing the effect on earnings behavior since the logarithm of negative values is not defined.[41] On the other hand, as has been highlighted by Banker and Byzalov (2014), the linear model requires more careful screening of the data sample since it is more sensitive to outliers compared to the log model.

Balakrishnan, Labro, and Soderstrom (2014) suggest another specification of the ABJ model: namely, scaling with lagged sales rather than with total costs in order to control for the effects of fixed costs in the level model of cost stickiness.[42] Banker and Byzalov (2014) name further possible scales such as lagged assets, market or book value of equity.

Another specification of the ABJ model is provided by Banker et al. (2014). The authors conduct a two-period model, which explicitly incorporates managerial expectations for future sales based on prior sales decrease or sales increase. While

---

39 See Banker, Byzalov, and Chen (2013), p. 121.

40 Anderson, Banker, and Janakiraman (2003) repeat their estimations with the linear model of cost stickiness and arrive at qualitatively similar results.

41 See Banker and Byzalov (2014), p. 56.

42 The linear specification of Balakrishnan, Labro, and Soderstrom (2014) has obtained the name recognition as the linear ABJ model or Balakrishnan, Labro, and Soderstrom (2014) model (e.g., Banker and Byzalov 2014; Rouxelin, Wongsunwai, and Yehuda 2015).

the ABJ model only captures the weighted average of two distinct processes: cost stickiness conditional on prior sales increase and cost anti-stickiness conditional on prior sales decrease; the two-period model allows for the superior explanation and prediction of cost behavior by explicitly incorporating prior sales changes.[43]

2.3.2 The Model of Weiss (2010)

Other than the ABJ model, the model of Weiss (2010) provides a firm- and period-specific measure of cost stickiness.[44] For this purpose, Weiss (2010) considers the costs and sales changes of a firm's last four quarters, where the calculations are based on the data from the most recent quarter with sales decrease and the recent quarter with sales increase. For the selected quarters Weiss (2010) builds the difference of the logarithmized ratios of cost changes:

$$STICKY_{i,t} = -\left[log\left(\frac{\Delta COST}{\Delta SALE}\right)_{i,\underline{\tau}} - log\left(\frac{\Delta COST}{\Delta SALE}\right)_{i,\overline{\tau}}\right] \qquad 2.3$$

$$with\ \underline{\tau}, \overline{\tau} \in \{t, \dots, t-3\},$$

where $\underline{\tau}$ is the most recent of the last four quarters with a decrease in sales and $\overline{\tau}$ is the most recent of the last four quarters with an increase in sales, $\Delta SALE_{i,t} = SALE_{i,t} - SALE_{i,t-1}$, $\Delta COST_{i,t} = (SALE_{i,t} - EARNINGS_{i,t}) - (SALE_{i,t-1} - EARNINGS_{i,t-1})$, and $EARNINGS$ is income before extraordinary items.[45] Thus, a lower measure of STICKY implies more sticky cost behavior and is consistent with the stickiness measure β_2 in the ABJ model used in Eq. 2.2. Similar to the ABJ model, the logarithmic measure is motivated by comparability across firms and mitigation of potential heteroscedasticity.

Weiss (2010) calculates the cost stickiness measure based on the total costs for two reasons. First, he examines the effect of asymmetric cost behavior on the accuracy of analysts' earnings predictions, which rely on estimation of total costs. Second, applying total costs rather than different cost components eliminates the problem of managerial discretion as regards cost classification (Anderson and Lanen 2009). Nevertheless, the cost measure of Weiss (2010) can be estimated for different cost

43 See Banker et al. (2014), p. 229.

44 The ABJ model can be also implemented for measuring cost stickiness at the firm level by using the time-series regression model. One disadvantage of this approach is the data loss. Anderson, Banker, and Janakiraman (2003) estimate the individual time-series models for firms that have at least 10 observations and three or more sales decreases during the sample period. Another disadvantage is that a firm's degree of stickiness is not periodic-specific.

45 See Weiss (2010), p. 1447.

components. For instance, Rouxelin, Wongsunwai, and Yehuda (2015) calculate the cost stickiness measure for the sum of SG&A and COGS costs to proxy for labor costs and Weiss (2010) uses SG&A and COGS to check for the consistency with other literature.

The applicability of Weiss's sticky measure leads to a loss of observations in periods where sales and earnings move in the opposite direction, due to the assumption that costs increase with the activity level increase. Another data loss arises when a firm exhibits strict sales decreases or strict sales increases in four successive quarters.[46] Despite certain limitations, Weiss's cost stickiness model offers a wide range of empirical analysis since it first, makes it possible to classify firms into sticky and anti-sticky, thus enabling the separate analysis for subsamples and, second, allows for the examination of asymmetric cost behavior as an explanatory variable on other outcomes.

To summarize, both the ABJ model and Weiss's model have their advantages and deficiencies, therefore the choice of the stickiness model as well as their variation depends crucially on the research question.

2.4 Empirical Research in Asymmetric Cost Behavior

Generally, empirical research on cost stickiness can be categorized into three main groups: empirical evidence on the existence of cost stickiness (Section 2.4.1), empirical evidence on the determinants of cost stickiness (Section 2.4.2) and, finally, empirical evidence on the consequences of cost stickiness (Section 2.4.3).

2.4.1 Empirical Evidence on the Existence of Cost Stickiness

A large body of research literature documents asymmetric cost behavior across multiple datasets distinguishing at the aggregation level. In this section I present the main findings of empirical evidence of cost stickiness occurrence across different cost categories (Section 2.4.1.1) as well as across various aggregation levels from department-specific to country-specific (Section 2.4.1.2).

---

46 To avoid this data loss, the estimation window can be extended to, for example, 8 or 12 quarters, while calculating the average cost sticky measure on a rolling basis would limit the effect of statistical outliers.

2.4.1.1 *Asymmetric Cost Behavior of Different Cost Categories*

Anderson, Banker, and Janakiraman (2003) provided the first comprehensive empirical evidence for asymmetric cost behavior, detecting stickiness of SG&A costs. Their results initiated a broad range of empirical studies finding evidence of asymmetric behavior of other cost types. Detecting stickiness of different cost categories mitigates the concern of potential distortion caused by various cost classifications among companies (Subramaniam and Weidenmier 2003). In addition, Cannon (2014) provides evidence of asymmetric cost behavior using physical input quantities (aircraft seat-miles) to measure activity. Banker and Byzalov (2014) highlight the importance of physical quantities and physical activity measures when documenting cost stickiness since it alleviates the assertion that *"cost stickiness could be an artifact of price changes or accruals manipulations"*.[47]

Table 2.1 provides an overview of empirical studies documenting the sticky behavior of different cost categories.

Table 2.1: Stickiness of different cost components

Study	Cost Type
Anderson, M. C., R. D. Banker, and S. N. Janakiraman. 2003. Are Selling, General, and Administrative Costs "Sticky"? *Journal of Accounting Research* 41 (1): 47-63.	SG&A costs
Subramaniam C. and M. L. Weidenmier. 2003. *Additional Evidence on the Sticky Behavior of Costs.* Working Paper, Texas Christian University.	SG&A costs, COGS, Total costs (SG&A+COGS), R&D costs, Advertising costs
Banker, R. D. and L. Chen. 2006a. *Labor Market Characteristics and Cross-Country Differences in Cost Stickiness.* Working Paper, Temple University, Georgia State University.	Operating expenses defined as sum of COGS and SG&A costs
Calleja, K., M. Steliaros, and D. C. Thomas. 2006. A Note on Cost Stickiness: Some International Comparisons. *Management Accounting Research* 17 (2): 127-140.	Total operating costs

[47] Banker and Byzalov (2014), p. 50.

Balakrishnan, R. and T. Gruca. 2008. Cost stickiness and core competency: A note. *Contemporary Accounting Research* 25 (4): 993-1006.	Operating costs (total costs associated with patient care and general facility operations, i.e., labor costs and costs for direct nonmedical supplies and purchased services)
Anderson, S. W. and W. N. Lanen 2009. Understanding Cost Management: What Can We Learn from the Evidence on 'Sticky Costs'? Working Paper, Rice University, University of Michigan.	SG&A costs, Total costs (SG&A +COGS), Labor costs, R&D costs
Dierynck, B., W. R. Landsman, and A. Renders. 2012. Do managerial incentives drive cost behavior? Evidence about the role of the zero earnings benchmark for labor cost behavior in Belgian private firms. *The Accounting Review* 87 (4): 1219-1246.	Labor costs
Kama, I. and D. Weiss. 2013. Do Earnings Targets and Managerial Incentives Affect Sticky Costs? *Journal of Accounting Research* 51 (1): 201-224.	Operating costs (annual sales revenue minus income from operations)
Balakrishnan, R., E. Labro, E., and N. S. Soderstrom. 2014. Cost Structure and Sticky Costs. *Journal of Management Accounting Research* 26 (2): 91-116.	SG&A costs
Banker, R. D., Byzalov, D., Ciftci, M., and R. Mashruwala. 2014. The Moderating Effect of Prior Sales Changes on Asymmetric Cost Behavior. *Journal of Management Accounting Research* 26 (2): 221-242.	SG&A costs, COGS, Advertising costs, R&D costs
Cannon, J. N. 2014. Determinants of "Sticky Costs": An Analysis of Cost Behavior using United States Air Transportation Industry Data. *The Accounting Review* 89 (5): 1645-1672.	Aircraft capacity costs (sum of depreciation, aircraft rental, maintenance,

	landing fees, and capacity purchase agreement expenses)

2.4.1.2 *Asymmetric Cost Behavior at Different Levels*

The majority of the cost stickiness literature focuses on data at the firm level. One of the few exceptions to this is the study of Balakrishnan and Gruca (2008), already mentioned in Section 2.2, which examines sticky costs within a firm, at department level. Balakrishnan and Gruca (2008) document sticky cost behavior in the departments directly related to patient care (surgical suites, in-patient wards) and thus contributing to the hospital's core competency. However, they do not find sticky costs in the ancillary (e.g., pharmacy and therapy) and support services (e.g., laundry, dietics, hospital administration or building maintenance).[48] Balakrishnan and Gruca (2008) attribute their result mainly to the higher adjustment costs associated with the core operations and to the hospital's social responsibility.[49]

The occurrence of cost stickiness has also been documented in single industries such as: health care (Noreen and Soderstrom 1994), air transportation (Cannon 2014), banking (Porporato and Werbin 2012), farming (Argilés and García-Blandón 2009), merchandizing, service, and manufacturing (Subramaniam and Weidenmier 2003; He, Teruya, and Shimizu 2010).

Subramaniam and Weidenmier (2003) investigate the degree of cost stickiness in each industry as well as the industry-specific differences focusing on merchandizing, service, financial, and the manufacturing industry. Thereby, they investigate fixed asset intensity, employee intensity, inventory intensity, industry concentration intensity, and the tenor of sales decline as major determinants of cost stickiness. The authors observe SG&A stickiness in manufacturing, merchandising and service industries, and COGS stickiness in the manufacturing, financial and (only marginally) service industries. The highest level of stickiness in SG&A costs is exhibited by manufacturing firms as a result of their high levels of fixed assets and inventory, while the lowest level of stickiness is observed in merchandising and service industries due to their low levels of fixed assets. Further, the determinants of sticky cost behavior differ across industries. For instance, the main driver of

48 Differentiation between the three groups is based on the ranking of departments in terms of their contribution to the core competency (see Balakrishnan and Grusha 2008, p. 996).

49 As discussed in Section 2.2.1.1, sticky costs may occur as a result of a firm's policy, which is not necessary motivated by value maximizing.

stickiness in merchandising and service is inventory intensity, whereas the manufacturing industry is mostly influenced by fixed asset intensity. Overall, the findings of Subramaniam and Weidenmier (2003) demonstrate that the occurrence of asymmetric cost behavior in various industries is justified by the adjustment cost explanation and that the major determinants differ across industries.

The empirical evidence for cost stickiness occurrence has been further documented in various countries. Table 2.2 presents an overview of selected studies providing evidence of cost stickiness prevalence in different countries.

Table 2.2: Country-specific prevalence of cost stickiness

Study	Country
Anderson, M. C., R. D. Banker, and S. N. Janakiraman. 2003. Are Selling, General, and Administrative Costs "Sticky"? *Journal of Accounting Research* 41 (1): 47-63.	USA
De Medeiros, O. R. and P. de Souza Costa. 2004. *Cost Stickiness in Brazilian Firms.* Working Paper, University of Brasilia.	Brazil
Balakrishnan, R. and T. Gruca. 2008. Cost stickiness and core competency: A note. *Contemporary Accounting Research* 25 (4): 993-1006.	Canada
Argilés, J. M. and J. García-Blandón. 2009. Cost stickiness revisited: empirical application for farms. *Spanish Journal of Finance an Accounting* 38 (144): 579-605.	Spain
He, D. S, J. Teruya, and T. Shimizu. 2010. Sticky Selling, General, and Administrative Cost Behavior and its Changes in Japan. *Global Journal of Business Research* 4 (4): 1-10.	Japan
Uy, A. O. O. 2011. Modeling Cost Behavior: Linear Models for Cost Stickiness. *Academy of Accounting and Financial Studies Journal* 15 (1): 25-34.	The Philippines
Dierynck, B., W. R. Landsman, and A. Renders. 2012. Do managerial incentives drive cost behavior? Evidence about the role of the zero earnings benchmark for labor cost behavior in Belgian private firms. *The Accounting Review* 87 (4): 1219-1246.	Belgium
Porporato, M. and E. Werbin. 2012. Evidence of sticky costs in banks of Argentina, Brazil and Canada. *International Journal of Financial Services Management* 5 (4): 303-320.	Argentina, Brazil, Canada

Abu-Serdaneh, J. 2014. The Asymmetrical Behavior of Cost: Evidence from Jordan. *International Business Research* 7 (8): 113-122.	Jordan
Bradbury, M. E and T. Scott. 2015. *Do managers understand asymmetrical cost behaviour?* Working Paper, Massey University and University of Auckland.	New Zealand
Bugeja, M., M. Lu, and Y. Shan. 2015. Cost stickiness in Australia: Characteristics and determinants. *Australian Accounting Review* 25 (3): 248-261.	Australia
Bu, D., C. Wen, and R. D. Banker. 2015. Implications of asymmetric cost behavior for analyzing financial reports of companies in China. *China Journal of Accounting Studies* 3 (3): 181-208.	China
Ibrahim, A. E. A. 2015. Economic growth and cost stickiness: Evidence from Egypt. *Journal of Financial Reporting and Accounting* 13 (1): 119-140.	Egypt
Lee, S. Y. 2015. Cost behavior during the global financial crisis: The case of Korean commercial banks. *Asia-Pacific Journal of Multimedia Services Convergent with Art, Humanities, and Sociology* 5 (2): 387-394.	Korea

While the studies listed in Table 2.2 examine cost stickiness in a single manner, others investigate the differences in asymmetric cost behavior across multiple countries, providing more insights into the sources of sticky costs.

For instance, Calleja, Steliaros, and Thomas (2006) conduct an international comparison across Germany, the USA, the UK and France and find evidence for sticky cost behavior for every single country as well averaged across all the firms. Further, Calleja, Steliaros, and Thomas (2006) document a higher degree of cost stickiness in German and French firms compared to UK and US firms. The authors attribute their result to the differences in the systems of corporate governance and in the level of external oversight of management behavior. In the common law countries, here the UK and US, corporate governance is characterized by its emphasis on the shareholder interests rather than other stakeholders. In addition, the stock market plays a significant role as external pressure on managerial decisions in the interests of shareholders. In contrast, in code-law countries such as Germany or France, the corporate governance system prioritizes the interests of a wide range of stakeholders. Further, the stock market plays significantly lesser role in the German and French financial systems compared to the UK and US. These factors may mean that managers are inclined to maintain unutilized resources by an activity level decrease.[50] In summary, Calleja, Steliaros, and Thomas (2006) explain the differences across the code-law and common law countries by variations in the level of adjustment costs. Thereby, the question as to whether the main driver of higher cost stickiness in Germany and France is attributable to adjustment costs, and thus economically driven, or whether this is due to legal restrictions,[51] which cannot be influenced by management, remains unclear.

In a similar manner, Banker, Byzalov, and Threinen (2013) investigate cross-country differences in asymmetric cost behavior. Comparing cost behavior of 20 countries, the authors document a higher degree of cost stickiness in countries with i) high judicial efficiency and ii) a high level of development, where the countries with iii) high shareholders' protection exhibit lower degree of cost stickiness. With respect to judicial efficiency (i), Banker, Byzalov, and Threinen (2013) argue that managers from countries with high judicial efficiency operate with greater confidence since their contracts will be enforced with fairness and alacrity, with any illegal or extra-legal expropriation being less likely. Therefore, Banker, Byzalov, and Threinen (2013) expect that managers from countries with high judicial efficiency are more willing to undertake major commitments of resources that have high adjustment costs. Consequently, high judicial efficiency is positively associated with cost stickiness. Concerning the level of a country's development (ii), Banker, Byzalov, and Threinen (2013) explain that more developed countries have more human capital intensive jobs and are therefore confronted with a higher level of labor adjustment costs. Therefore, a firm's degree of cost stickiness increases with the level of its country's development. Lastly, with respect to the strength of a country's shareholder protection (iii), Banker, Byzalov, and Threinen (2013) justify their prediction based on the agency problem associated with empire building. As discussed in Section 2.2.1.2 above, empire-building managers will avoid downward resource adjustment by a sales decline. Strong shareholder protection is expected to mitigate this agency problem, thus the strength of shareholder protection law is negatively associated with the degree of cost stickiness.

In sum then, comprehensive research can be said to provide strong evidence of asymmetric cost behavior as a worldwide phenomenon, occurring across various cost categories, departments, companies, industries and countries.

---

50 See Calleja, Steliaros, and Thomas (2006), p. 129.

51 I discuss the unavoidable cost stickiness occurrence due to the legal restrictions in Section 2.2.2, on p. 11.

2.4.2 Empirical Evidence of the Cost Stickiness' Determinants

As shown in Section 2.2, cost stickiness may have multiple explanations for its occurrence. Empirical tests necessarily require empirical proxies for the tests of theoretical predictions. Table 2.3 provides an overview of the selected empirical proxies for cost stickiness determinants.

Table 2.3: Determinants of cost stickiness

Determinants	Effect	Authors
Adjustment costs		
Asset intensity	+	Anderson, Banker, and Janakiraman (2003) Banker and Byzalov (2014)
Bargaining power of unions proxied by trade union density (percentage of all wage and salary earners that are trade union members)	+	Banker and Chen (2006a)
Employee intensity	+	Anderson, Banker, and Janakiraman (2003) Banker and Byzalov (2014)
Employment protection legislation strictness	+	Banker, Byzalov, and Chen (2013)
Intangible assets	+	Venieris, Naoum, and Vlismas (2015)
Inventory intensity	+	Subramanian and Weidenmier (2003)
Product differentiation strategy	+	Banker, Flasher, and Zhang (2014)
Managers expectations (future sales expectations)		
GDP growth	+	Anderson, Banker, and Janakiraman (2003) Banker et al. (2014) Banker and Byzalov (2014)
Order backlog	+	Banker et al. (2014)
Successive sales decreases	-	Subramanian and Weidenmier (2003)

		Banker and Byzalov (2014)
Successive sales increases	+	Banker et al. (2014)

Behavioral explanation		
Overconfidence measure based on CEOs' option exercise behavior	+	Chen, Gores, and Nasev (2013)
Overconfidence measure based on prominence of CEO's photograph	+	Qin, Mohan, and Kuang (2015)
Empire building		
CEO horizon (number of years manager is expected to remain in company)	+	Chen, Lu, and Sougiannis (2012)
CEO tenure	+	Chen, Lu, and Sougiannis (2012)
CEO compensation	+	Chen, Lu, and Sougiannis (2012)
Free Cash Flow	+	Chen, Lu, and Sougiannis (2012) Banker and Byzalov (2014)
Earnings management incentives		
Loan approval	-	Banker and Fang (2013)
Small profit, i.e., $0 \leq$ net income / total assets at the beginning year < 1%	-	Dierynck, Landsman, and Renders (2012)
Small profit, i.e., $0 \leq$ net income before extraordinary items / market capitalization at the beginning year < 1%	-	Kama and Weiss (2013)
Small profit, i.e., $0 \leq$ net income / market capitalization at the beginning year < 1%	-	Banker and Byzalov (2014)

Small earnings increases, i.e., 0 ≤ (net income - preceding net income) / market value at the beginning year < 1%	-	Kama and Weiss (2013) Banker and Byzalov (2014)
Mechanical		
Technological constrains	+	Kama and Weiss (2010)

2.4.3 Empirical Evidence of the Cost Stickiness' Implications

As has been pointed out by Banker and Byzalov (2014), the model of Weiss (2010) is especially advantageous when studying the potential consequences of asymmetric cost behavior by using Weiss's sticky measure as an explanatory variable. While the pre 2010 cost stickiness literature focused on its occurrence, determinants and main drivers, the post 2010 period is characterized by a growing, but still modest, number of studies that examine cost stickiness' implications for other areas. The urgent need for academic research providing valuable recommendations to practices in contrast to understanding the process of decision-making is highlighted by Krishnan (2015). Thus, the following section considers empirical studies of asymmetric cost behavior's consequences.

Study of Banker and Chen (2006b)

Banker and Chen (2006b) examine the impact of cost stickiness on earnings forecasts by developing a model that incorporates cost stickiness and cost variability. Thereby, the authors rely on empirical findings from, inter alia, Fairfield, Sweeney, and Yohn (1996) that show that separating earnings into their components with different levels of persistence reduces the forecast error for earnings forecasts. The alternative approach of earnings decomposition provided by Banker and Chen (2006b) is based on firms' production processes, i.e., those components proportional to sales changes and others that are unrelated to a sales decrease or sales increase. In other words, earnings are defined as revenues less fixed (i.e., unrelated to sales changes) and variable (proportional to sales decrease or increase) expenses. This decomposition makes it possible to consider interdependency between sales and costs and therefore the incorporation of asymmetric cost behavior. By using a sample of 4,348 firms in the period from 1992 to 2002, Banker and Chen (2006b) document that their novel model outperforms other prediction models in forecasting one-year-ahead returns on equity. Other models include one simple forecast model based only on past return on equity and two established prediction models based on the earnings decomposition into operating and non-operating components (Fairfield, Sweeney, and Yohn 1996), and into operating and non-operating income components (Sloan 1996). Banker and Chen (2006b) conclude that capital market earnings expectations are better represented by an earnings forecast model, which incorporates cost variability and cost stickiness, addressing the question of the extent to which the market recognizes asymmetric cost behavior over a longer horizon to further research.

Study of Anderson, Banker, Huang, and Janakiraman (2007)

Anderson et al. (2007) reconsider the interpretation of SG&A costs to sales ratio,[52] a signal used to fundamental analysis. According to the traditional view of fundamental analysis, a change in SG&A ratio between two periods is considered as a measure of operating efficiency and ability to control costs.[53] An increase in SG&A ratio demonstrates operating inefficiency and managements' inability to control costs, where a decrease constitutes the opposite.[54] Since managerial ability or inability to control costs persists in future periods (Lev and Triagarian 1993), the increase in SG&A ratio is interpreted as a negative signal concerning future profitability. Anderson et al. (2007) highlight that the traditional interpretation is based on the implicitly made assumption, that SG&A costs should change proportionately with sales.[55]

Anderson et al. (2007) build on the insights of Lev and Triagarian (1993): a signal may have different implications for future earnings and crucially depends on additional information. The authors use a sales decrease or, respectively, a sales increase as additional support in interpretation of SG&A ratio changes. Anderson et al. (2007) argue that an increase in SG&A ratio in revenue-declining period can be attributed to i) fixity, ii) stickiness of SG&A costs or iii) managers' failure to control costs. With respect to i), a higher SG&A ratio caused by fixity of costs in a period with a sales decrease would imply expectations of higher future earnings rather than managerial inefficiency, since future earnings are more positive for firms with a higher fraction of fixed SG&A costs to sales when the distribution of revenue over time has a positive drift.

With respect to ii), an increase in SG&A ratio caused by stickiness arises from the managers trading off the costs of maintaining redundant resources with adjustment costs. Thus, an increase in SG&A ratio caused by asymmetric cost behavior during the revenue decreasing period signals positive managerial expectations about future

52 Hereafter SG&A ratio.
53 See, for instance, Bernstein (1988), p. 682.
54 See Lev and Triagarian (1993), p. 196.
55 See Anderson et al. (2007), p. 3.

revenue development and is therefore associated with higher future earnings. While an increase in SG&A costs due to stickiness and fixity represents a positive association with future earnings, managerial inability to control costs (iii) would provide negative information about future earnings.

Based on the sample comprising 23,002 firm-year observations from 1983 to 2002, Anderson et al. (2007) estimate an earnings prediction model, which incorporates the fixity and stickiness of SG&A costs, and document that future earnings are positively related to the change in SG&A ratio and that abnormal positive returns can be earned by investing in firms with high increases in the SG&A ratio during the periods of falling sales.[56]

Study of Baumgarten, Bonenkamp, and Homburg (2010)

Baumgarten, Bonenkamp, and Homburg (2010) build on the results of Anderson et al. (2007), by distinguishing between firms with intended and unintended SG&A ratio increase. An increase is considered as intended by management if a firm's SG&A ratio is below the industry average in the previous period, and as unintended otherwise. The former firms are classified as cost-efficient firms, the latter as cost-inefficient. Using the sample of 5,524 firms with 26,102 firm-year observations from 1984 to 2005, Baumgarten, Bonenkamp, and Homburg (2010) find evidence of a positive impact of intended SG&A ratio increase on future earnings. The authors attribute their results to the ability of cost-efficient firms to lower the future cost of goods sold, and thus consider the SG&A expenditures of cost-efficient firms as partial investments in operating efficiency.

In an additional analysis Baumgarten, Bonenkamp, and Homburg (2010) show that although the stickiness model of Anderson et al. (2007) has an impact on future earnings, the effect is weaker compared to their model.[57] Moreover, the authors find no empirical evidence on the positive relation between SG&A expenditures and future sales and question the sticky explanation of the SG&A ratio's ability to generate future earnings, an argument used by Anderson et al. (2007).

Study of Weiss (2010)

Weiss (2010) analyzes how analysts' earnings forecasts are influenced by asymmetric cost behavior. For this purpose, he develops a new measure of cost stickiness at the firm level, which allows for the classification of firms as sticky or

56 Anderson et al. (2007) calculate the abnormal returns adjusted for size and book-to-market risk.
57 See Baumgarten, Bonenkamp, and Homburg (2010), Table 5.

anti-sticky.[58] Based on the sample of 44,932 industrial firm quarters for 2,520 firms from 1986 to 2005, Weiss (2010) documents a negative relation between cost stickiness and accuracy of earnings forecasts. More precisely, the mean absolute analyst consensus earnings forecast error is equal to 0.0080 for sticky firms, where the error of forecasts for anti-sticky firms amounts to 0.0060. Weiss (2010) attributes less accurate earnings forecasts for sticky firms to their lower earnings predictability.

Further, Weiss (2010) examines how the extent of analyst coverage is influenced by sticky cost behavior. He argues that if analysts recognize the relationship between asymmetric cost behavior and the accuracy of earnings forecasts, cost stickiness will affect analysts' coverage priorities. Indeed, Weiss (2010) finds evidence of a negative statistically significant influence of cost stickiness on analysts' coverage.

Finally, Weiss (2010) examines whether investors understand asymmetric cost behavior, building on the findings of Abarbanell, Lanen, and Verrecchia (1995), who document that forecast precision increases the earnings-price response coefficient.[59] Weiss (2010) claims that, if investors recognize that firms with stickier costs tend to have less predictable earnings, then investors will rely less on reported earnings leading to a weaker market response to earnings surprises for firms with stickier cost behavior. As postulated, Weiss (2010) finds evidence for investors' recognition of cost stickiness with respect to total cost, but not for the stickiness of cost components such as COGS and SG&A costs.

Study of Rouxelin, Wongsunwai, and Yehuda (2015)

Rouxelin, Wongsunwai, and Yehuda (2015) examine how aggregate cost stickiness affects the future macro-level unemployment rate. Since firms with asymmetric cost behavior are less inclined to terminate employees when the activity level falls, the authors expect a lower future unemployment rate in the short run. Thereby, the authors measure cost stickiness as average cost stickiness across all firms in a given quarter, where the sum of COGS and SG&A costs is used as a proxy for labor costs.

Rouxelin, Wongsunwai, and Yehuda (2015) argue that cost stickiness can predict the future unemployment rate because of the two types of information contained in the aggregate cost stickiness measure: i) the magnitude of adjustment costs associated with labor costs such as hiring or firing costs and ii) managerial expectations about future sales and thus the product and labor markets.

---

58 The details of Weiss' model are presented in Section 2.3.2.

59 The earnings-price response coefficient measures the sensitivity of price change to an earnings surprise (see Abarbanell, Lanen, and Verrecchia 1995, p. 41).

Using the sample of US firms in the period from 1990 through 2012 Rouxelin, Wongsunwai, and Yehuda (2015) document that a one-standard-deviation higher cost stickiness in recent quarter results in a 0.6 to 0.8 percentage point lower unemployment rate over the next four quarters.

Study of Ciftci, Mashruwala, and Weiss (2016)

Ciftci, Mashruwala, and Weiss (2016) investigate the extent to which analysts incorporate cost variability and cost stickiness in forecasting future earnings. The authors argue that if analysts recognize cost behavior to its full extent, then there would be no systematic relationship between cost behavior and earnings forecasts errors. To test this hypothesis empirically, Ciftci, Mashruwala, and Weiss (2016) consider the ratio between the earnings forecast error and sales forecast error under favorable (high demand) and unfavorable (low demand) scenarios. The authors note that since the earnings forecast error is the sum of the sales and expenses forecast error, the considered ratio measures the direct impact of the expense prediction error on the earnings forecast error.[60]

Ciftci, Mashruwala, and Weiss (2016) demonstrate that if analysts estimate fixed costs, the asymmetric cost response to sales decreases, and cost variability correctly, then the ratio of earnings forecast error to sales forecast error would be equal under favorable and unfavorable scenarios. On the other hand, if analysts do not fully incorporate cost stickiness or cost variability in their forecasts, the prediction error yields differential degree of earnings forecast errors between favorable and unfavorable sales surprises of equivalent amount.

Using a sample of 105,577 firm-quarter observations between 1998 and 2011, Ciftci, Mashruwala, and Weiss (2016) document an asymmetric association between analysts' sales forecasts and earnings forecast errors: earnings forecasts errors are significantly higher with a negative sales surprise than with a positive sales surprise.

2.5 Criticism

Although the theory of asymmetric cost behavior introduced by Anderson, Banker, and Janakiraman (2003) has been widely accepted in the research community, selected studies provide contrary claims against the findings of sticky costs and criticize the theory underlying the ABJ model.

---

60 See Ciftci, Mashruwala, and Weiss (2016), p. 63.

Anderson and Lanen (2009) attribute three major critical arguments against the theory and methodology applied by Anderson, Banker, and Janakiraman (2003). First, the authors question the cost stickiness occurrence as a single conclusion of deliberate managerial decisions, i.e., as a result from active cost management. More precisely, Anderson and Lanen (2009) emphasize that the empirical evidence of asymmetric cost behavior is insufficient to discriminate between managerial cost management and mechanistic changes in cost and invoke researchers to take a closer look at managers who make resource adjustment decisions.[61] Second, Anderson and Lanen (2009) criticize the incorporation of "unusual" observations, i.e., observations in which costs and sales move in opposite directions, since it is inconsistent with the cost adjustment theory. When Anderson and Lanen (2009) repeat the analysis excluding the unusual observations, they still face sticky cost behavior but with a significantly lower coefficient.[62]

Banker, Byzalov, and Plehn-Dujowich (2011) address the concern of including unusual observations in their simulation analysis. First, the authors clarify that observations for which sales and costs move in opposite directions are not so unusual and are consistent with optimal cost management.[63] Second, Banker, Byzalov, and Plehn-Dujowich (2011) show that the approach of Anderson and Lanen (2009), i.e., discarding unusual observations, suffers from severe selection bias and can generate erroneous findings of no stickiness in a sample with substantial cost stickiness.[64] Banker and Byzalov (2014) also criticize the approach of Anderson and Lanen (2009) of deleting the observations with opposite changes in costs and sales but retaining the observations with rapidly declining costs, leading to biased estimates. Moreover, Banker and Byzalov (2014) name another source of potential bias, namely the incorrect screening procedure for costs exceeding sales, resulting in a large downward bias in cost stickiness.[65]

The third critical point raised by Anderson and Lanen (2009) refers to the inability of the ABJ model to detect asymmetric cost behavior for other cost categories such

---

61 See Anderson and Lanen (2009), p. 5.

62 The coefficient is equal to -0.2105 (-0.0139) in the sample including (excluding) unusual observations (see Anderson and Lanen 2009, Table 8).

63 Banker, Byzalov, and Plehn-Dujowich (2011) consider an example in which sales are declining in current period, but are expected to increase in subsequent periods. In this case, management will build up the resources leading to an unusual observation in the manner of Anderson and Lanen (2009): costs increase and sales decrease in a period.

64 More specifically, according to Banker, Byzalov, and Plehn-Dujowich (2011) the sample consisting of prevailing sales decreases will overestimate cost stickiness, where the sample with prevailing sales increases will underestimate cost stickiness. In their simulation data sales increases constitute almost two thirds of the whole sample, leading to cost stickiness underestimation when excluding unusual observations.

65 For details see Banker and Byzalov, pp. 59-60.

as advertising costs or physical resource measures (e.g., number of employees). Banker, Byzalov, and Plehn-Dujowich (2011) address this concern and confirm the results by documenting no stickiness for the number of employees by using the ABJ model. However, the authors do confirm sticky behavior when applying the extended two-period model of Banker et al. (2014). Banker, Byzalov, and Plehn-Dujowich (2011) conclude that a more complex pattern of stickiness and anti-stickiness (as expounded in the two-period model) must be considered if interdependencies behind the changes in the number of employees are to be understood.[66] With regard to other cost categories, Banker, Byzalov, and Plehn-Dujowich (2011) counter that the theory of sticky cost behavior does not necessarily imply stickiness of all types of cost categories, and thus cannot be expected of cost types with low adjustment costs such as advertising costs.

More recently, Balakrishnan, Labro, and Soderstrom (2014) question sticky costs theory in the presence of fixed costs. The authors argue that past managerial decisions affect the cost structure of a firm resulting in lower cost elasticity, which therefore induces slowed cost adjustment. This is misinterpreted as evidence of cost stickiness. Indeed, Balakrishnan, Labro, and Soderstrom (2014) find a significant impact of fixed costs on the degree of cost stickiness. Banker and Byzalov (2014) take up the fixed cost argument and criticize the crucial assumption of Balakrishnan, Labro, and Soderstrom (2014), which is a priori restrictive. More precisely, Balakrishnan, Labro, and Soderstrom (2014) assume the traditional model of fixed and variable costs thereby neglecting the underlying economic elements of this differentiation: fixed and variable costs arise from resources with exaggerated and marginal adjustment costs.[67] According to Banker and Byzalov (2014), the assumption regarding the costs of being either fixed or variable excludes the existence of resources with significant but not unaffordable adjustment costs. Further, Banker and Byzalov (2014) argue that even though fixed costs can produce average cost stickiness, the traditional cost model can be rejected based on empirical findings in asymmetric cost literature such as anti-sticky conditional on a prior sales decrease (Banker et al. 2014). Moreover, the fixed cost argument is inconsistent with the empirical findings of variation in degree of cost stickiness.[68]

The final concern of Balakrishnan, Labro, and Soderstrom (2014) relates to the log-log specification that produces a bias in favor of documenting sticky costs in the presence of fixed costs due to the non-constant cost response to activity changes.

---

66 See Banker, Byzalov, and Plehn-Dujowich (2011), p. 14.

67 See Banker and Byzalov (2014), p. 60.

68 Since the fixed cost argument is based on mechanistic cost functions, it predicts no effect of e.g., GDP growth or asset intensity on the degree of cost stickiness.

The authors demonstrate that the degree of cost stickiness is close to zero when they use the sales-deflated linear model, i.e., account for fixed costs.

As response to the above criticism, Banker and Byzalov (2014) reproduce the empirical analysis of Balakrishnan, Labro, and Soderstrom (2014) by using standard selection criteria and document robust and significant cost stickiness. Further, they show theoretically and empirically that the estimates change significantly because of the non-standard selection criteria of Balakrishnan, Labro, and Soderstrom (2014).[69]

In sum then, while the contradicting studies certainly raise appropriate concerns with respect to the empirical findings for asymmetric cost behavior, Banker, Byzalov, and Plehn-Dujowich (2011) as well as Banker and Byzalov (2014) demonstrate in their theoretical and empirical analysis that these objections are not justified, thereby validating the theory of asymmetric cost behavior.

---

69 Balakrishnan, Labro, and Soderstrom (2014) discard observations for which current SG&A costs exceed prior period sales.

3 Theoretical Foundations of Credit Risk Fundamentals and Methods of Determining Credit Risk

This chapter provides fundamentals of credit risk underlying the rest of my thesis. Section 3.1 introduces the term “credit risk” and provides a classification of credit risk into various risk categories. In Section 3.2, I discuss credit risk measurement based on two theoretical models: structural and reduced-form approaches. In Section 3.3, I proceed with the measurement of credit risk, whereby the credit derivative CDS is considered in detail. Figure 3.1 illustrates the structure of this chapter.

Figure 3.1: Structure of Chapter 3

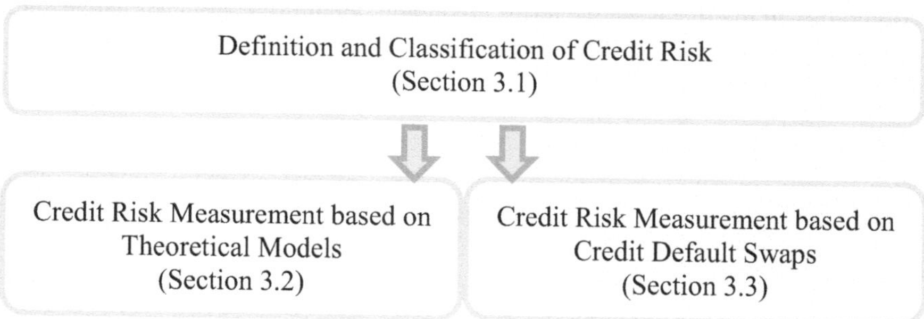

3.1 Definition and Classification of Credit Risk

Understanding credit risk and its interaction with general risk is of utmost relevance. The classic credit risk literature defines credit risk as *“the risk of default or of reductions in market value caused by changes in the credit quality of issuers or counterparties”*,[70] while the definition of risk in general, provided in the 1920s by the Encyclopedia Britannica, continues to maintain its pertinence today and describes risk as the *“hazard, chance of danger or loss”*.[71]

---

70 Duffee and Singleton (2003), p. 4.
71 Garvin (1929), p. 322.

K. Reimer, *Asymmetric Cost Behavior*, Quantitatives Controlling,
https://doi.org/10.1007/978-3-658-22822-4_3

The research literature offers various ways to categorize risks, whereby typical classifications are based on the clustering according to the risks' characteristics or sources. Since the definition of credit risk implies that this may occur if and only if the position is an asset, I present risk categorization from a bank's perspective. The total risk of a financial institution can be divided into credit, market, liquidity, operational, legal and regulatory, and human factor risk.[72] One possibility to classify credit risk is based on its definition. Thus, credit risk can be subdivided into *default* and *migration* risk. Default risk refers to that which arises from the counterparty's actual insolvency, i.e., inability to repay its debt obligations.[73] Migration risk on the other hand describes the risk of loss resulting from deterioration in the credit quality, hence reducing the market value of a credit exposure.[74] In contrast to default risk, which measures risk at the current point of time, migration risk measures risk not only over a period of time but also considers future periods. The literature often uses the terms "default risk" and "credit risk" as synonyms, corresponding to the credit risk definition in a narrow sense. I apply this terminology in my thesis, so the terms credit and default risk are interchangeable. Figure 3.2 illustrates the presented classification of bank's financial risks.

72 The focus of this thesis is on credit risk. For a detailed explanation of other financial risk categories see Crouphy, Galai, and Mark (2001), p. 34-39 or Duffee and Singleton (2003), p. 3-6.

73 See Resti and Sironi (2007), p. 277.

74 See Crouphy, Galai, and Mark (2001), p. 316.

Figure 3.2: Categories of Bank's Financial Risk

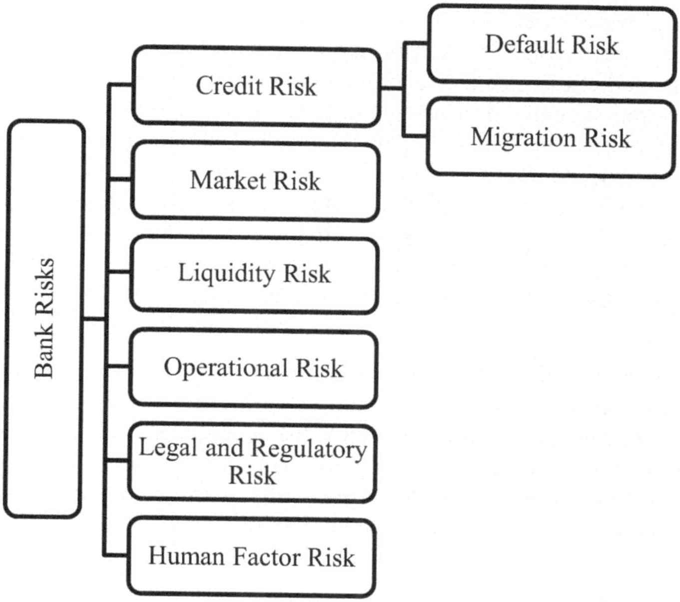

Source: Own design based on Grouphy, Galai, and Mark (2001), p. 35 and Schlecker (2009), p. 12.

3.2 Credit Risk Measurement based on Theoretical Models

In essence, the finance literature offers two types of theoretical models to estimate the pricing of credit derivatives. The classical approaches of *structural models* are essentially based on the work of Black and Scholes (1973) and Merton (1974). This term is reasoned by the focus of these models on the *structural* characteristics of a firm that determine its probability of default, i.e., the values of assets and the volatility of asset values.[75] In contrast, the *reduced-form models* concern the default of a firm exogenously and are based on the historical statistical data of default experience by credit class.[76]

75 See Resti and Sironi (2007), p. 322.
76 See Resti and Sironi (2007), p. 403.

3.2.1 Structural Models

In a seminal paper, Merton (1974) proposed an option pricing approach to the valuation of credit risk. The Merton model assumes a risk-neutral world with frictionless markets, i.e., no transaction costs, no taxes, infinitely divisible assets, continuous trading, equal borrowing and lending rate, allowed short-sales, and a sufficient number of investors.[77] To distinguish risk structure from term structure effects on pricing, Merton (1974) further assumes a "flat" term structure with a known instantaneously risk-free interest rate (r_f) constant over time. The firm value (V_t) is specified as a stochastic process with log normal distribution, under which the variance of the firm's rate of return is constant. In addition, the capital structure of a firm is simplified and comprises equity and a single zero-coupon debt (*D*),[78] maturing on date *T*.

Under these assumptions Merton (1974) formulates a model in which a firm can default at maturity of the debt obligation when the firm value of assets is insufficient to meet the promised amount to the debt holders. The credit risk arises from the probability of asset value being less than debt obligation ($V_T < D$).[79] Figure 3.3 illustrates the distribution of the assets' value at time T and the probability of default which is equal to the shaded area below D.[80]

77 See Merton (1974), p. 450 for the assumptions and Galai and Masulis (1976) for a detailed discussion of the assumptions.

78 A zero-coupon debt implies that all payments including the interest and the nominal value are realized at the end of the contract (see Hull 2006, p. 80).

79 As already shown, credit risk is unequal to default risk. Nevertheless, the Merton model treats credit risk as default risk constituting thereby one of its shortcomings.

80 It is important to note that this figure illustrates a risk-neutral world, whereas in a risky world the assets follow a drift.

Figure 3.3: The Intuition behind the Merton Model

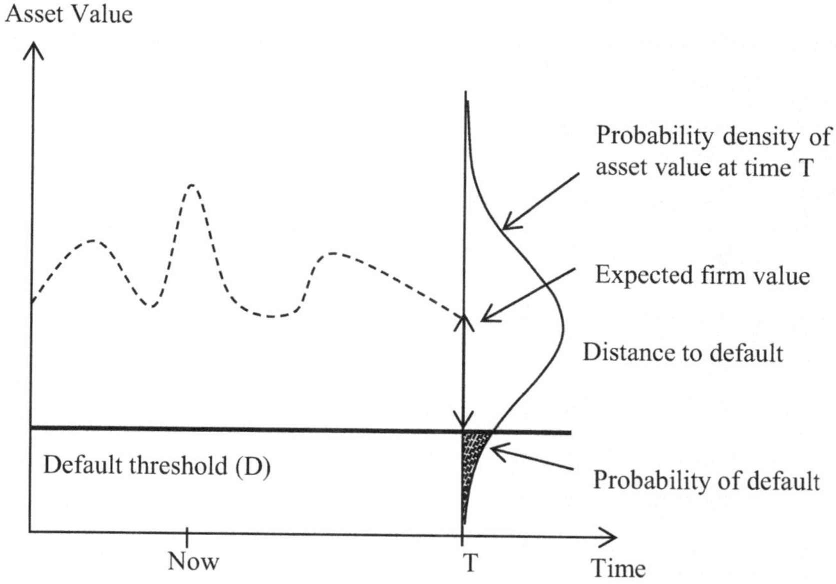

At the maturity of debt obligation, the debt holders receive the repayment amount or the value of the firm if D exceeds V_T, formally: min $\left\{V_T, D\right\}$ or $D - \max\left\{D - V_T, 0\right\}$.[81] Thus, a debt holder's claim is equivalent to the portfolio comprising a default-risk-free bond paying D at time T and a short put option on the firm's assets with strike D.[82]

In other words, the debt holders will recover D for certain, but the equity holders can exercise the right of paying the firm in exchange, whenever $V_T > D$.[83] Consequently, the market value of a risky debt (B^*) is the difference between the value of the default-risk-free bond (B)[84] and the value of the put option (P):

81 The notation and the model's presentation are based on Sundaram and Das (2016), pp. 803-811.

82 The short put option obliges the writer to purchase the underlying asset by a certain day at a certain price (see Hull 2006, p. 6).

83 See Sundaram and Das (2016), p. 803 for the next paragraph.

84 For simplicity, hereafter I refer to a default-risk-free as a risk-free bond or rather, debt.

$$B^* = B - P. \tag{3.1}$$

The value of risk-free debt can be easily obtained by discounting the face amount D due at T at the riskless rate r_f:

$$B = e^{-r_f(T-t)}D. \tag{3.2}$$

The price of the put option can be derived by applying the Black-Scholes formula:[85]

$$P = e^{-r_f(T-t)}DN(-d_2) - V_tN(-d_1), \tag{3.3}$$

where

$$d_1 = \frac{1}{\sigma\sqrt{T-t}}\left[ln\left(\frac{V_t}{D}\right) + \left(r_f + \frac{1}{2}\sigma^2\right)(T-t)\right] \tag{3.4}$$

$$d_2 = d_1 - \sigma\sqrt{T-t}. \tag{3.5}$$

$N(\cdot)$ is standardized cumulative density function, D is the strike price of the option (face value of the debt), T is maturity of the option (date of the debt's redemption), r_f is the risk-free rate, V_t the market price of the underlying assets (asset value or equivalently firm value), σ is the standard deviation of returns on the underlying assets (s.d. of returns on the asset value).[86]

Merton (1974) defines the leverage ratio (L) as the ratio of the present value of the debt to the total firm's value:[87]

$$L = \frac{e^{-r_f(T-t)}D}{V_t}. \tag{3.6}$$

Then, he formulates d_1 and d_2 as a function of leverage:[88]

85 See Black and Scholes (1973), p. 647.

86 The interpretation of $N(d_1)$ or $N(d_2)$ and especially d_1 or d_2 is not trivial and the detailed investigation would go beyond the scope of this thesis. While Merton (1974) and Black and Scholes (1973) do not explain or interpret the probability factors $N(d_1)$ and $N(d_2)$, other research papers focus specifically on the interpretation of these terms (e.g., Nielsen 1993).

87 See Merton (1974), p. 454.

88 See Appendix 1 for the deviation of d_1 and Appendix 2 for the deviation of d_2.

$$d_1 = \frac{ln\left(\frac{1}{L}\right) + \frac{1}{2}\sigma^2(T-t)}{\sigma\sqrt{T-t}} \quad 3.7$$

$$d_2 = \frac{ln\left(\frac{1}{L}\right) - \frac{1}{2}\sigma^2(T-t)}{\sigma\sqrt{T-t}} = d_1 - \sigma\sqrt{T-t}. \quad 3.8$$

The value of the firm's risky debt can be determined by inserting the value of the put option defined in 3.3 as well the value of the discounted riskless debt defined in 3.2 into 3.1:

$$\begin{aligned} B^* &= e^{-r_f(T-t)}D - e^{-r_f(T-t)}DN(-d_2) + V_tN(-d_1) \\ &= e^{-r_f(T-t)}D[1 - N(-d_2)] + V_tN(-d_1) \\ &= e^{-r_f(T-t)}D\left[N(d_2) + \frac{V_tN(-d_1)}{e^{-r_f(T-t)}D}\right] \quad 3.9 \\ &= e^{-r_f(T-t)}D\left[N(d_2) + \frac{1}{L}N(-d_1)\right] \end{aligned}$$

with L, d_1, and d_2 defined in 3.6, 3.7, and 3.8 respectively.

The debt's yield or yield to maturity r^* (i.e., the discount rate that equalizes the present value of the face value and the current value of the debt) can now be derived from the following equation:[89]

$$B^* = e^{-r^*(T-t)}D. \quad 3.10$$

Rearranging and substituting 3.1 for B^* and 3.2 for B results in:

$$r^* = -\frac{1}{(T-t)}ln\frac{B^*}{D} = -\frac{1}{(T-t)}ln\left(\frac{e^{-r_f(T-t)}D - P}{D}\right). \quad 3.11$$

Finally, the default spread can be determined as the difference between yield to maturity and the risk-free rate. Inserting the derived above value of the put option (Eq. 3.3) and some simplifications yield Merton's risk premium (*credit spread*):

89 See Resti and Sironi (2007), p. 326.

$$r^* - r_f = -\frac{1}{(T-t)} ln\left[N(d_2) + \frac{1}{L}N(-d_1)\right] \quad 3.12$$

with L, d_1, and d_2 defined in 3.6, 3.7, and 3.8 respectively.[90]

The Eq. 3.12 shows that for a given maturity, the default spread is a function of only the variance of the firm's assets and the leverage (i.e., the ratio of the discounted at the risk-free rate nominal value of the debt to the current value of the firm).[91]

Partial derivatives allow theoretical statements to be made on the relationships between the risk premium and the determinants of the option prices, formally:[92]

$$\frac{\partial(r^*-r_f)}{\partial\sigma^2} > 0; \frac{\partial(r^*-r_f)}{\partial L} > 0; \frac{\partial(r^*-r_f)}{\partial r_f} < 0;$$
$$\frac{\partial(r^*-r_f)}{\partial V_t} < 0; \frac{\partial(r^*-r_f)}{\partial T} \gtrless 0. \quad 3.13$$

Eq. 3.13 demonstrates that the credit spread is an increasing function of asset variance, and leverage ratio and a decreasing function of risk-free rate and firm value, where the partial derivative with respect to maturity shows an inconclusive result.[93]

The considerations presented above are of a theoretical nature and do not necessary become evident in the empirical research. Largely, the divergence between the theoretical statements and the empirical results is caused by the restrictive assumptions and therefore practical difficulties in implementing the Merton model. One of the most significant limitations is that the market value of the debt required for the calculation of asset value as well as its volatility is not directly observable, since the capital structure of a firm is complex and often comprises forms of financing that have no liquid secondary market.[94]

90 See Merton (1974), p. 454 for the final equation and detailed deviation in the Appendix 3.

91 See Merton (1974), p. 454.

92 Merton (1974) presents the partial derivatives of the risk premium with respect to leverage, maturity, and variance. More detailed comparative static analysis can be found in Schlecker (2009), pp. 74-76.

93 More precisely: for a leverage ratio $\geq$1, the risk premium is a decreasing function of maturity; for the leverage ratio < 1, the credit spread increases first and then decreases with the maturity (see Merton 1974, p. 459).

94 See Crouphy, Galai, and Mark (2001), pp. 395-396 and Resti and Sironi (2007), p. 330-332 for a detailed discussion of limitations.

A significant number of research papers provide enhancements and extensions of Merton's work building a range of structural models.[95] One of the most extensive empirical examinations of structural models is performed by Eom, Helwege, and Huang (2004). The authors investigate the ability of structural models, especially Merton (1974), Geske (1977), Longstaff and Schwartz (1995), Leland and Toft (1996) and Collin-Dufresne, Goldstein, and Martin (2001) to predict corporate bond spreads. The authors document that the models of Merton (1974) and Geske (1977) underestimate the credit spreads, where the underestimation error in the model of Geske (1977) is significantly lower. Eom, Helwege, and Huang (2004) attribute this to the fact that the latter apply a compound option approach to coupons.[96] Even though the firm is actually insolvent, the shareholders may pay the coupon by selling new equity when they assess a good chance of improving their current position. The bondholders are exposed to a greater risk of loss since they recover less than they would at the outset of distress (i.e., before new equity selling).[97]

In contrast, the models of Leland and Toft, Longstaff and Schwartz, and Collin-Dufresne and Goldstein tend to overestimate credit spreads. Eom, Helwege, and Huang (2003) conclude that the crucial challenge to enhance the fit of structural models is to increase the average predicted spread relative to the Merton (1974) model without overvaluing the spreads of high volatility or high leverage firms.

3.2.2 Reduced-Form Models

In contrast to structural models, which model the default risk dependent on a firm's value and its capital structure, reduced-form models consider a firm's default as a random occurrence without reference to the firm's economic situation. Therefore, the parameters referring to the firm's value need not be estimated to implement reduced-form models.[98] Rather, the assumptions of a default process per se have to be made: the firm's default time and the recovery in the event of default are exogenously given processes, which are based on the information available to the market.[99]

---

95 For a survey of structural models see Das and Singleton (2003).

96 Compound options are options on options (see Geske 1979, p. 63).

97 The intuition behind these considerations is that the equity selling often marks the beginning of a downward spiral. The shareholders anticipate the dilution and begin to sell, resulting in a lower asset value. Thus the debt holders are exposed to greater risk since the asset value declines (see Eom, Helwege, and Huang 2004, p. 514).

98 See Altman, Resti, and Sironi (2004), p. 187.

99 See Jarrow (2011), p. 4.

The first reduced-form model was formulated by Bierman and Hass (1975).[100] Prominent enhancements include e.g., Jarrow and Turnbull (1995), Jarrow, Lando and Turnbull (1997), Lando (1998), and Duffie and Singleton (1999).[101] The basic idea of reduced-form models is that a risk-neutral investor will be indifferent when choosing between a risk-free government bond and a risky bond if the present value of the expected cash flows from a corporate bond discounted at a risk-free rate is equal to the price of government bond.[102]

While the expected cash flow from a government bond is per assumption default-risk-free and therefore equal to the promised payoffs, the expected value of the corporate bond's cash flows have to be determined under the consideration of default probability and recovery rate at default:[103]

$$B_0 = \sum_{t=1}^{T} \frac{q^{t-1}[q \cdot c + (1-q) \cdot \gamma \cdot (c + 100\%)]}{(1 + r_T^f)^t} + \frac{q^t \cdot 100\%}{(1 + r_T^f)^T} \qquad 3.14$$

with:

B_0 = price of defaultable bond matured in T

q = survival probability

c = coupon payment

γ = recovery rate

r_T^f = yield to maturity of a default-risk-free bond.

Next, the yield to maturity can be determined using the present value formula of the defaultable bond:[104]

$$r_T^d = \frac{1 + r_T^f}{q + \gamma - q \cdot \gamma} - 1\,, \qquad 3.15$$

where r_T^d is yield to maturity of a defaultable bond and other variables as defined in Eq. 3.14.

---

100 See Yawitz (1977), p. 484.

101 For a survey of the general characteristics of different reduced-form models, see Altman, Resti and Sironi (2004).

102 See Jonkart (1979), pp. 256-257.

103 See Schlecker (2009), p. 81.

104 See Yawitz (1977), p. 484.

The credit spread is calculated as the difference between the return of the defaultable bond and the government bond of the same maturity:[105]

$$cs = r_T^d - r_T^f \tag{3.16}$$

$$\begin{aligned} &= \frac{1 + r_T^f}{q + \gamma - q \cdot \gamma} - 1 - r_T^f \\ &= \frac{1 + (1 - \gamma) \cdot (1 - q) \cdot r_T^f}{q + \gamma - q \cdot \gamma} - 1, \end{aligned} \tag{3.17}$$

where cs is the credit spread and other variables are definied in Eq. 3.14.

Reduced-form models are usually implemented for the valuation purposes of credit derivatives and offer some advantages towards structural models. Debt prices make it possible to obtain information about the default intensity that is used to evaluate comparable credit derivatives. Thus, no traded equity price is required and the credit risk of private firms can be determined. Further, since reduced-form models do not rely on the asset value process, they can be used in a broader manner such as in the valuation of sovereigns.[106]

The major disadvantage of reduced-form models lies in the futility of using them to gain insights into fundamental determinants of credit spreads.[107] However, the empirical performance of reduced-form models in pricing risky bonds (e.g., Duffie and Singleton 1999; Jarrow, Li, Liu, and Wu 2010) and credit derivatives (e.g., Longstaff, Mithal, and Neis 2005; Longstaff and Rajan 2008) is fairly convincing.

Compared to the performance of structural models, there is no common agreement in academia or practice as to which framework explains credit risk better. In their recent study, Gündüz and Uhrig-Homburg (2014) provide an empirical investigation of structural and reduced-form models applying comparable estimation techniques to the same data set, where the quality of the models is assessed based on their ability to explain CDS prices. The authors document that both approaches underpredict CDS prices with an average of 21-26 basis points.[108] The models' predictive power is fairly close to average, with an outperformance of structural approach for shorter maturities and sub-investment grade CDSs and an outperformance of reduced-form approach for investment-grade CDSs and longer

---

105 For the detailed deviation see Yawitz (1977).

106 See Sundaram and Das (2011), p. 829.

107 See Collin-Dufresne, Goldstein, and Martin (2001), p. 2179.

108 See Gündüz and Uhrig-Homburg (2014), p. 54.

maturities. The authors conclude that the modeling type is irrelevant at the aggregate level compared to the input data used.

3.3 Credit Risk Measurement based on Credit Default Swaps

Apart from the measurement of credit risk premium based on theoretical models such as structural or reduced-form models presented in Sections 3.2.1 and 3.2.2 respectively, the credit risk can be determined by observing the market prices of credit derivatives. The most popular credit derivative is the credit default swap, which I consider in more detail in the following.[109]

3.3.1 Definition and Structure of Credit Default Swap

Credit Default Swap is a contract between two counterparties, the protection seller and the protection buyer. A CDS contract can be thought of as insurance against the risk of default by a particular company (*reference entity*).[110] The protection buyer, the holder of the CDS pays a periodical payment to the protection seller until the contract's end or the occurrence of a credit event, whichever comes first.[111] The credit events, e.g., bankruptcy, downgrade in the rating, restructuring are defined by the International Swaps and Derivatives Association (ISDA), a trade organization in the Over-The-Counter (OTC) market acting to standardize the credit derivatives.[112] This periodical payment is called *CDS premium* or *CDS spread* and is defined as a percentage of the *notional amount*, expressed in basis points. The CDS contract distinguishes two kinds of *settlement*. Under the physical delivery, the protection buyer provides the bond to the protection seller in exchange for the nominal value (*par value*). The cash settlement of the underlying asset implies the payment amounting to the difference between the par value and the market value of the bond immediately after the credit event or a predetermined recovery fraction.[113] Figure 3.4 illustrates the interdependencies between two counterparties in a CDS contract.

---

109 According to the Bank of International Settlement (BIS) at the end of June 2016, CDSs add up to almost 99% of overall credit derivative market (see BIS 2016, p. 13).

110 See Hull (2006), p. 507.

111 See Longstaff, Mithal, and Neis (2005), p. 2214.

112 See Resti and Sironi 2007, p. 464.

113 See Longstaff, Mithal, and Neis (2005), p. 2217 or Crouphy, Galai, and Mark (2001), p. 453.

Figure 3.4: Payment Structure of a Credit Default Swap

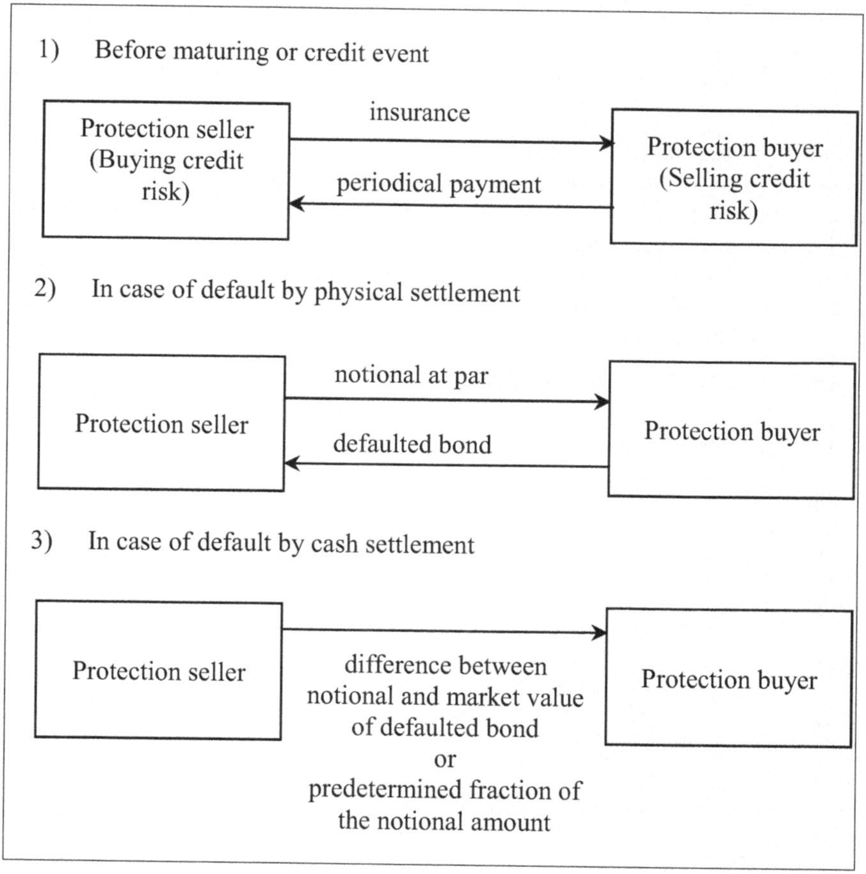

3.3.2 Credit Default Swap Market

Since 1994, the year of creation of CDSs by J.P. Morgan, the CDS market has experienced enormous growth. The main sources for the CDS surveys are: i) the Bank for International Settlements; ii) the International Swap and Derivatives Association; and iii) the Depository Trust & Clearing Corporation. The numbers among the data providers may differ due to different sampling and collection methods as shown by ISDA (2008).

The market size is usually measured by *notional amount outstanding*, since these data are easily identified and gathered.[114] The nominal or notional amount outstanding is defined as the value of all deals concluded and not yet settled on the reporting date,[115] or equivalently, it is the sum of all derivatives contracts being bought or sold in terms of nominal values.

According to the Bank for International Settlements, the size of the CDS market amounted to about $6 trillion at the end of 2004 and continued its exponential growth up to the financial crisis of 2007. At the end of 2007 the market size of the CDS market in terms of gross notional amounts outstanding[116] reached a peak of $58 trillion, which constituted 10% of the global OTC derivatives markets. Figure 3.5 presents the global gross notional amounts outstanding in the CDS market in the period from 2004 to 2016.[117]

Figure 3.5: CDS Notionals Outstanding ($bn)

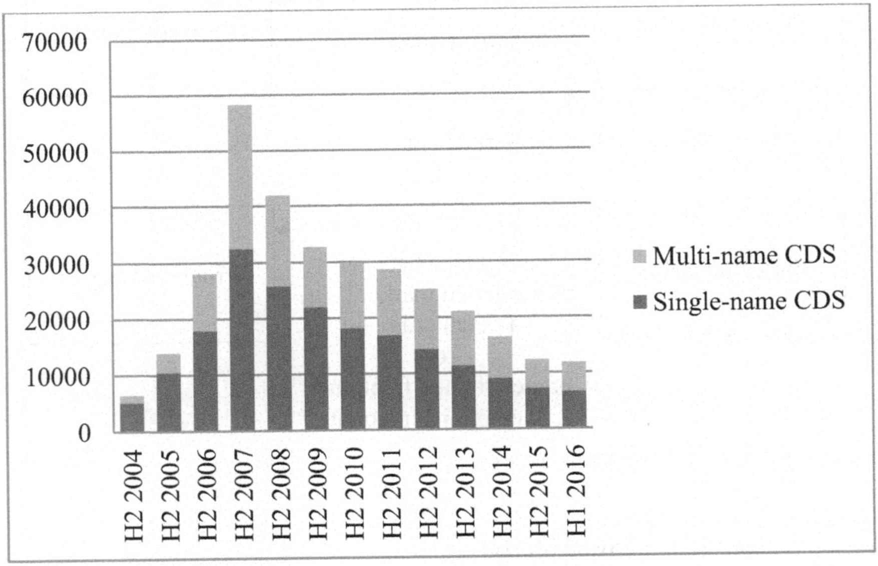

Source: BIS Semiannual OTC Derivatives Statistics

114 See ISDA (2008), p. 2.

115 See BIS (2015), p. 4.

116 The term gross indicates that contracts with positive and negative values with the same counterparty are not netted (see BIS 2015, p. 5).

117 The time range is based on data availability at www.bis.org.

Figure 3.5 further dissects the CDS market statistics by contract type. While the single-name CDS is protection against a predefined credit event of one reference entity, the multi-name CDS offers protection against the credit event of more than one entity. The multi-name CDSs comprise Index CDSs, Tranched Index CDSs, and Basket CDSs.

Single-name CDSs remain the most important instruments with an average share of 62% in the considered time. Compared to 2004, the ratio of multi-name CDSs to total CDSs more than doubled in 2007 (from 20% to 44%) and ranged after this time between 33% in 2009 and 46% in 2013. Weistroffer (2009) attributes the growing popularity of multi-name CDSs to the increased index trading for trading purposes as well for proxy hedges when a direct hedge of one certain reference is not available.

Another measure of CDS market size is provided by outstanding derivative contracts in terms of *gross market values*, defined as the sum of all outstanding derivative contracts, with either positive or negative replacement values calculated at market prices. Replacement value represents price, which could be received or paid if the contract were to be sold. In other words, if a quoted price is available then the market value is a product of trading units and quoted price, otherwise it is estimated by the price of a similar contract or by applying a valuation model such as discounted cash flow.[118] Similar to market size measure in terms of notional amounts outstanding, market values can be expressed on a gross or net basis, which simply takes into account bilateral netting.[119]

Further, gross market values provide information on the scale of market risk in derivatives trades as well as economic significance.[120] Figure 3.6 below illustrates the CDS market development in terms of market values. Unfortunately, BIS does not provide net notional amounts, where net market values are only available from 2011. Nevertheless, compared to the peak at the end of 2007 in terms of gross notional amounts outstanding (Figure 3.5), the peak of CDS market values on a gross basis was reached at the end of 2008, when credit protection was most valuable, namely after the outbreak of worldwide financial crisis and the default of Lehman Brothers.

---

118 See BIS (2015), p. 5.

119 Suppose that a bank Y purchases a credit protection from bank X for $50 million and then sells it to bank Z. The gross notional amount outstanding as the sum of all credit protection being sold or bought is equal to $100 million, where the net notional amount remains equal to $50 million. In the case of default bank Z receives $50 million from bank X.

120 See BIS (2016), p. 21.

Figure 3.6: CDS Market Values ($bn)

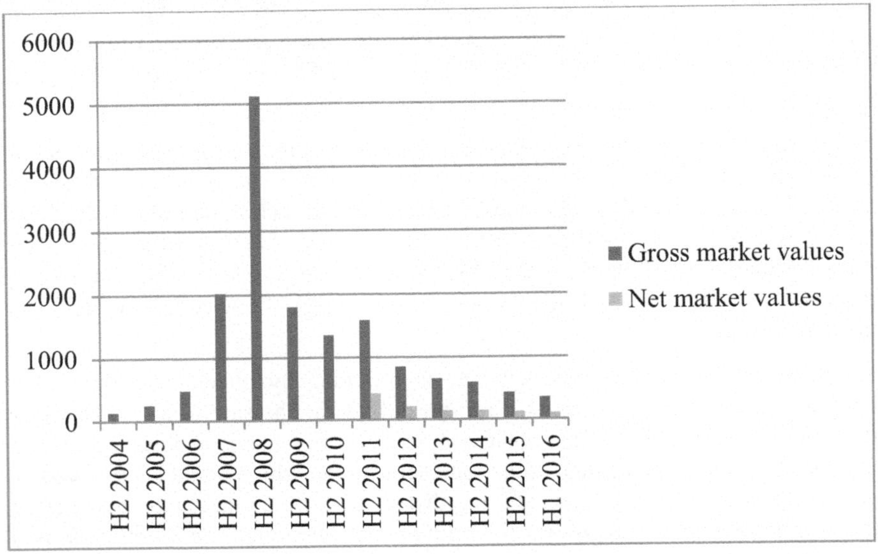

Source: BIS Semiannual OTC Derivatives Statistics

In contrast to absolute numbers presented above in Figures 3.5 and 3.6, Figure 3.7 illustrates the relative importance of the CDS market with regard to the global OTC derivatives market. Among credit derivatives the OTC market comprises foreign exchange, interest rate, equity-linked, and commodity contracts as well as other derivatives. CDSs experienced a remarkable rise until the financial crisis and reached almost 10% of the total volume in the global OTC market. At the end of first half of 2016 the CDS market represented a small proportion of 2.16% of $600 trillion OTC derivatives market.

Figure 3.7: Relative CDS Market Size

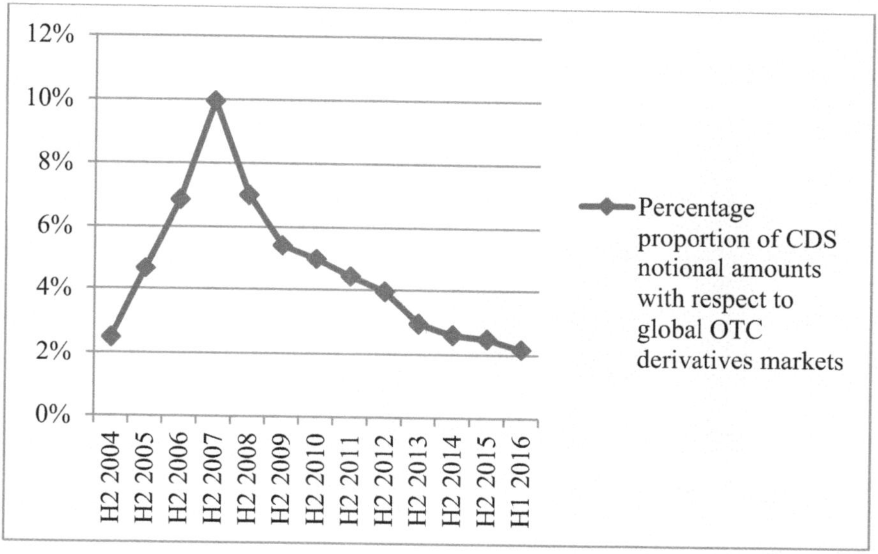

Source: BIS Semiannual OTC Derivatives Statistics

While the fraction of the CDS market with regard to the overall OTC derivatives market accounts on average to 4.61%, Figure 3.8 provides evidence that CDSs are the most important instrument among credit derivatives. According to the comprehensive market survey, which BIS conducts every three years, CDS attributed 88% in 2007 and 99% of overall credit derivatives market afterwards.

Figure 3.8: Credit Derivatives Notionals Outstanding ($bn)

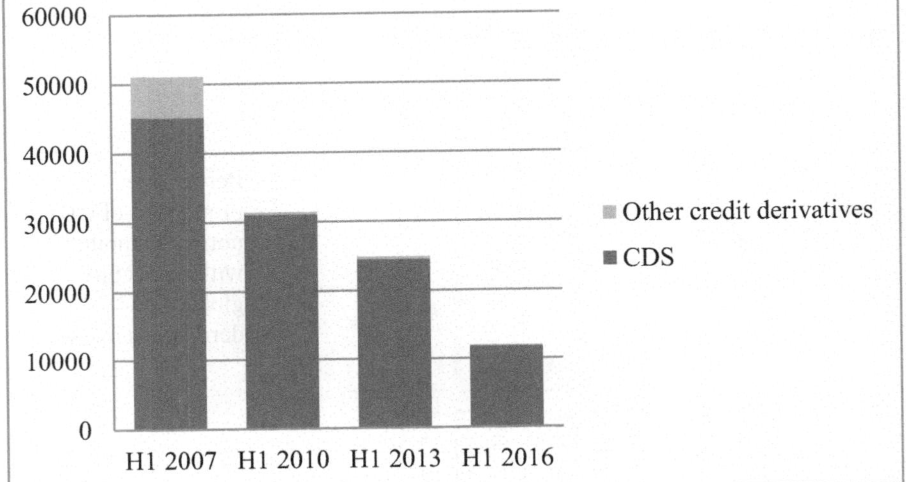

Source: BIS (2007) and BIS (2016)[121]

Further, the CDS contracts can be dissected based on the type of the reference entity into sovereign and non-sovereign CDSs. BIS (2015) defines sovereigns as "entities of a country's central, state or local government, excluding publicly owned firms and international organisations."[122] Accordingly, the non-sovereigns are any entities that do not belong to the category of sovereigns. Although non-sovereign contracts constitute the majority of the overall CDS market with an average fraction of about 90%, the proportion of sovereign credit derivatives' notional amounts outstanding to the overall CDS market rose almost continuously from 3.97% in 2008 to 16.28% in 2015.[123]

The growing trading of sovereign contracts may be explained by the increased hedging needs for sovereign issuers, but there is also a sign of speculative trading due to the fact that trading volumes almost doubled between 2010 and 2012 during the European sovereign debt crisis (Augustin, Subrahmanyam, Tang, and Wang 2014).

121 The BIS provides the more comprehensive survey on a triennial basis, which, besides CDSs, also contains other credit derivative instruments such as forwards and swaps as well as options. The data for CDSs are available from the first term of 2007 with a gap of three years.

122 BIS (2015), p. 15.

123 Calculations are made based on the publicly available data at www.bis.org.

The overall trend in CDS market decline since 2008 can be primarily explained by *portfolio compression* and does not necessary imply a reduction in CDS trading activity (Vause 2010). Portfolio compression or trade compression describes a practice of reducing unnecessary counterparty exposure by offsetting claims between market participants.[124]

In sum, although the fact that the CDS market declined after 2007 in terms of notional amounts and represents a small fraction of global OTC market, it continues to be a highly sizable and important part of the credit derivatives market.

3.3.3 Credit Default Swaps and Credit Risk

As shown in Section 3.2, the credit spread measures the credit risk and is defined as the difference between risky bond yield spread and the risk-free rate assuming complete markets. In an arbitrage-free framework the difference between the risky bond yield spread and the CDS spread for the same company should be equal to zero (Duffie 1999).

Nevertheless it is possible to observe a difference empirically, known as the *CDS-Bond basis,* which simultaneously raises a question in an appropriate credit risk measure. Empirical research considers the CDSs as a pure credit risk measure, where CDSs' superiority in measuring credit risk is based mostly on the following considerations. First, the CDS market leads the bond and equity markets in price discovery. Price discovery is a process of incorporating new information into the asset prices through trading. The analysis of the effects of any credit relevant information on credit prices necessarily requires fast incorporation into asset prices especially for short-interval tests.[125] Second, the CDS spreads are directly observable. In contrast, the bond spreads rely on an appropriate choice of riskless rate, which can be problematic (Houweling and Vorst 2005). Third, the bond spreads contain non-default components such as tax (Elton, Gruber, Agrawal, and Mann 2001) or a liquidity premium (Longstaff, Mithal, and Neis 2005).

In following I present a summary of key empirical studies supporting the hypothesis of CDSs' superiority over other credit derivatives and provide additional insights as to why they measure credit risk more accurately.

Study of Norden and Weber (2004)

---

124 See Duffie, Li, and Lubke (2010), p. 4.

125 See Griffin (2014), p. 865.

Strategy: Norden and Weber (2004) analyze the response of a stock and CDS market to rating downgrades as well as reviews for downgrade by using the sample of daily 5-year CDS spread observations of 90 European, Asian, and US firms during the time period from 2000 to 2002. Applying event study methodology, the authors calculate for each event type mean abnormal stock returns (i.e., in excess to relevant stock market index) and mean adjusted CDS spreads changes (i.e., adjusted for the CDS index).

Results: Strong abnormal pre-announcement performance of stock and CDS markets can be recognized. While both markets anticipate the rating downgrades approximately 90 to 60 days before the announcement day, the anticipation of reviews for downgrade (usually preceding a rating change) starts earlier in the CDS market. Since CDS market participants act mostly for hedging and diversification purposes, the trading is more frequent and directly related to credit risk leading to a lesser proportion of noise traders in the CDS market. As an additional reason the authors mention the potential insider information from banks' creditors departments.

Study of Longstaff, Mithal, and Neis (2005)

Strategy: Longstaff, Mithal, and Neis (2005) analyze CDS prices and corporate spreads for 68 firms in the period from March 2001 to October 2002. The corporate spread is divided into default and non-default components (the difference between credit spread and default component). The default component is estimated either (i) by the CDS spreads or (ii) by applying the reduced-form models.

Results: The majority of credit spreads are due to default risk. The non-default component of corporate spreads is strongly related to bond illiquidity and slightly to the differential state tax treatment of bonds.

Study of Blanco, Brennan, and Marsh (2005)

Strategy: Blanco, Brennan, and Marsh (2005) examine the accuracy of credit risk pricing and efficiency in price discovery by analyzing CDS and bond spreads of 33 entities from January 2001 to June 2002. To examine the price discovery in the bond and CDS market, Blanco, Brennan, and Marsh (2005) apply common factor models of Hasbrouck (1995) and Gonzalo and Granger (1995). Hasbrouck's model understands price volatility as a reaction to new information and measures each market's contribution to the variance of the innovations to the common factors. The market with the highest relative contribution to this variance is considered to be superior in price discovery. In Gonzalo and Granger's framework the price discovery leadership is attributed to the market that adjusts least to price changes in other markets.

Results: On average the CDS and bond markets price credit risk over time in a similar manner. Strong evidence is documented that the CDS market leads the bond market in price discovery. The authors explain that the superiority is due to (i) the synthetic nature of CDSs enabling a convenient place for the trading of credit risk and (ii) the presence of more institutional, well informed traders in the CDS market compared to bond market.

Study of Zhu (2006)

Strategy: Zhu (2006) examines the efficiency in price discovery and the accuracy of credit risk pricing by analyzing daily quotes of CDSs and bonds of 24 entities in the period from January 1999 to December 2002. To examine the long-term co-movements of CDS and bond spreads, the cointegration test proposed by Engle and Granger (1987) is applied.[126] To analyze the short-term dynamic interactions between the two spreads, in particular the efficiency in price discovery, the author implements the framework of Gonzalo and Granger (1995).[127]

Results: In the long run there are no discrepancies between the CDS spreads and bond yields. In the short run the CDS market leads the bond market in price discovery; the price leadership is stronger in the US based companies. For certain firms that experienced credit shocks during the analyzed period, the price discrepancies in CDS and bond spreads are much higher. The author concludes that the superiority of the CDS market in price discovery is due to the higher responsiveness of CDS to changes in credit conditions.

3.3.4 Discussion of Credit Default Swaps' Applicability in Measuring Credit Risk

Despite the wide acceptance among researchers and practitioners of CDS in describing pure credit risk, empirical evidence suggests that the observed CDS spreads are too high in comparison to the premium predicted by theory (Berndt, Douglas, Duffie, Ferguson, and Schranz 2005; Pan and Singleton 2008). This

126 The test of Engle and Granger (1987) is based on the theorem of Granger (1981) which claims that when two time series follow an I (1) process (i.e., stationary only after differencing), it is possible that a linear combination of them follows an I (0) process (i.e., stationary without differencing) and those variables are co-integrated. To test whether the variables co-integrate, Engle and Granger (1987) introduce a two-stage framework, in which the ordinary least square regression is established and the unit root tests are applied to test for the stationarity of the residuals. The variables are stated as being long-term related if the residuals from the estimation are stationary.

127 More specifically, using the estimates from the vector error correction model, a ratio of the speed of adjustments with a range between 0 and 1 is calculated to measure the contribution of each market in price discovery (see Zhu 2006, p. 230).

difference implies the existence of non-default factors in the CDS premia and engendered a range of empirical studies examining the determinants of CDS spreads besides the default risk.[128]

For example, Tang and Yan (2007) document that both liquidity level and liquidity risk are significant factors in CDS contracts. Thereby, liquidity describes the degree to which assets can be traded quickly without affecting the asset's current price and the liquidity risk is the uncertainty associated with the liquidity level.[129] The intuition behind this relation is based on the higher costs associated with less liquid contracts such as search costs for the counterparty, compensation for the risk of trading against informed traders,[130] inventory costs of traders with funding constraints or other handling costs. Similarly, Bongaerts, De Jong, and Driessen (2011) document the liquidity premium earned by CDS sellers and develop a theoretical asset pricing model incorporating the liquidity risk.

Besides the effect of the liquidity, the risk of the counterparty's financial distress, *counterparty risk,* may also affect CDS pricing. In particular, when the default risk of the protection seller (i.e., the counterparty) increases, the value of the protection (i.e., the CDS contract) sold should decline.[131] Arora, Gandhi, and Longstaff (2012) find strong evidence that counterparty credit risk is priced in the CDS market, although the magnitude of the effect is decidedly small in economic terms.[132,133]

More generally, Lin, Liu, and Wu (2011) provide new CDS and bond pricing models with default and non-default components where the parameters of these models are obtained from pooled bond and CDS data. By formulating common default intensity for CDS and bonds, the authors are able to identify the default and non-default factors (as a difference between the CDS premium and the default component) of CDS, which on average explains 13% of the CDS premium.

Further, the contract specific features such as a restructuring clause or seniority level may also have influence on CDS pricing.[134] Therefore, the use of CDS as a credit measure in empirical research crucially requires either a homogenously

---

128 For a comprehensive survey of credit default swaps in general see Augustin et al. (2014); for an accounting related overview see Griffin (2014).

129 See Tang and Yan (2007), p. 7.

130 Acharya and Johnson (2007) provide evidence of informed trading in CDS markets.

131 See Arora, Gandhi, and Longstaff (2012), p. 286.

132 More precisely, an increase in protection seller's credit risk by 645 basis points leads on average to one-basis-point decrease in the price of credit protection.

133 Given the small economical effect of counterparty risk on CDS pricing, I do not consider the counterparty risk in the empirical investigation presented in Chapter 4.

134 I provide more details on this issue in Section 4.3.2.

compiled data set or model composition, which controls for contract specific characteristics.

The research on CDS and its determinants is becoming increasingly broader just as it faces the problem of model specification, omitted variable problems, or both. Nevertheless, the following observations can be derived from the current available research literature: although the CDS spreads contain (partly unidentified) non-default components, they are less affected than the bond spreads; the CDS market leads the equity and bond markets in price discovery; and finally, its relatively simple implementation in light of the direct observability of the CDS prices are convincing in considering CDSs as a useful credit risk transfer mechanism.

4 Does Cost Stickiness Affect Credit Risk?

In this chapter I conduct an empirical study, which investigates empirically the impact of asymmetric cost behavior on credit risk. In Section 4.2, I discuss the related literature and develop the research question. In Section 4.3, I describe the sample selection procedure, model specification, and variables measurement. I discuss the empirical results in Section 4.4, consider endogeneity in Section 4.5, document robustness in Section 4.6, and conclude in Section 4.7. Figure 4.1 illustrates the structure of this Chapter. [135]

Figure 4.1: Structure of Chapter 4

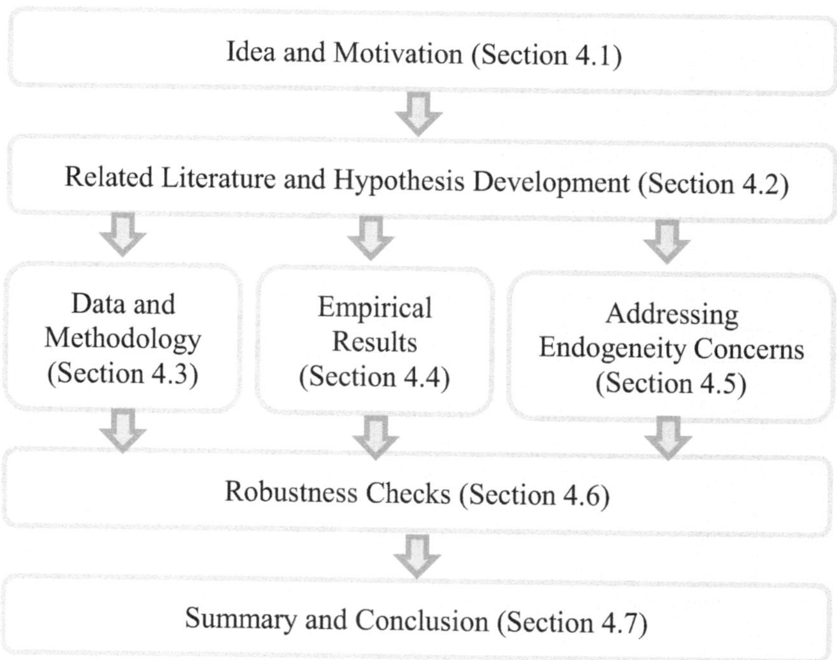

[135] This chapter is based on the working paper: Homburg, Nasev, Reimer, and Uhrig-Homburg 2016, *Does Cost Management Affect Credit Risk?* Even though I have written this paper together with Prof. Carsten Homburg, Jun.-Prof Julia Nasev, and Prof. Marliese Uhrig-Homburg I use the first person throughout this chapter to provide consistency within the doctoral thesis.

K. Reimer, *Asymmetric Cost Behavior*, Quantitatives Controlling,
https://doi.org/10.1007/978-3-658-22822-4_4

4.1 Idea and Motivation

Understanding cost behavior is important for corporate insiders and outsiders. Managers for example are motivated to actively manage costs because costs separate the top from the bottom line of the income statement and the bottom line is frequently used to evaluate managers' performance. In particular, when sales are difficult to influence and markets are very competitive, managers can focus on costs to improve profitability. Although corporate outsiders like investors, creditors, and financial analysts tend to focus more attention on large capital expenditures, they also care about operating expenditures and cost. This is because operating expenditures occur much more frequently and reflect the efficiency with which managers use resources including capital expenditure when running the business. Hence, one dimension outsiders use to evaluate managers and firm performance is management's ability to efficiently control costs.

While there is evidence that cost management affects important measures of firm performance, little is known about the impact of cost behavior on credit risk. This is surprising since theory and empirical evidence suggest that costs do not move mechanically with volume (e.g., sales) but tend to decline less when sales decrease than they rise with an equivalent sales increase. The main contribution of this study is to show that this asymmetric cost behavior, known as cost stickiness (Anderson, Banker, and Janakiraman 2003), increases corporate credit spreads.

I argue that cost stickiness can be interpreted as an investment in a risky project. In particular, when activity levels fall, managers face the dilemma of whether to adjust or keep redundant resources. Since future demand is uncertain, keeping unutilized resources is risky. If firms reduce costs less when sales fall compared to how they increase costs when sales increase earnings will be lower for sales declining periods and higher for sales increasing periods. This increases earnings variability (Weiss 2010) and hence ceteris paribus the probability of default.[136] Since higher earnings volatility also reduces earnings persistence and therefore earnings quality, its negative effect on credit risk might even be reinforced. A potentially offsetting effect could lie in a value-enhancement through the active cost management strategy. However, I do not expect this effect to be dominating and therefore predict that firms with higher levels of cost stickiness exhibit higher credit risk. To test this hypothesis, I use the sticky cost model of Weiss (2010) and measure credit risk with

136 For studies documenting that higher earnings or cash flow volatility increases credit risk see e.g. Francis, LaFond, Olsson, and Schipper (2005) and Jung, Soderstrom, and Yang (2013).

CDS spreads, which are commonly perceived as a relatively pure measure of credit risk (Ericsson, Jacobs, and Oviedo 2009; Tang and Yan 2007).[137]

My data comprises the intersection between Compustat, CRSP and Markit. Using a sample of 2,906 5-year CDS-quarters from 2001 to 2011 as well as a sample of 23,765 CDS-quarters including maturities from six months up to 30 years, I find that CDS spreads increase with cost stickiness after controlling for well-known credit default swap determinants. More specifically, a one standard deviation increase in cost stickiness increases the CDS premium by 27 basis points on average. This result is robust to different lag structures, variable measurement, and alternative empirical specifications.

I contribute to prior literature in several ways. To my knowledge this study is the first that examines the impact of cost behavior on credit risk, expanding the accounting literature on sticky costs (Anderson, Banker, and Janakiraman 2003; Anderson et al. 2007; Weiss 2010; Kama and Weiss 2013) by adding an implication for credit markets.

A large body of research has identified important characteristics and determinants of cost stickiness: e.g., firm-specific stickiness (e.g., Balakrishnan, Petersen, and Soderstrom 2004; Chen, Lu, and Sougiannis 2012; Kama and Weiss 2013; Cannon 2014), agency determinants of stickiness (e.g., Chen, Lu, and Sougiannis 2012; Dierynck, Landsman, and Renders 2012; Kama and Weiss 2013), and behavioral determinants of stickiness (e.g., Banker et al. 2014; Chen, Gores, and Nasev 2013). However, the number of studies examining consequences of cost stickiness is notably smaller. Prior studies have examined implications of cost stickiness such as its impact on future performance (Banker and Chen 2006b; Anderson et al. 2007; Baumgarten, Bonenkamp, and Homburg 2010), its impact on the accuracy of analysts' forecasts (Weiss 2010; Ciftci, Mashruwala, and Weiss 2016), and on unemployment rates (Rouxelin, Wongsunwai, and Yehuda 2015). I extend this literature by adding a new implication of cost stickiness.

My findings also add to the understanding of CDS pricing. Prior financial accounting studies show the relevance of earnings for credit risk (Das, Hanouna, and Sarin 2009; Callen, Livnat, and Segal 2009) and the ability of the combination of accounting based and market based models to explain variation in CDS spreads (Correia, Richardson, and Tuna 2012). I take a management accounting perspective and provide evidence for the relevance of asymmetric cost behavior for credit risk.

Finally, the documented negative credit market response to cost stickiness is also important in practice. On one hand, my finding can help creditors, analysts, and

[137] For detailed discussion of CDS' applicability in measuring credit risk refer to Section 3.3.4.

credit rating agencies to predict credit risk associated with asymmetric cost behavior. On the other hand, managers learn that failing to cut costs when demand declines increases their firms' credit risk and eventually their financing costs.

4.2 Related Literature and Hypothesis Development

Prior literature on firms' cost behavior documents economic, behavioral, and agency explanations for the cross-sectional variation in the degree of cost stickiness.[138] According to the economic explanation, managers refrain from reducing costs because of frictions in resource adjustment. In particular, when the decline in activity levels is considered as temporary, high costs of adjusting resources might make it attractive to keep redundant resources (Anderson, Banker, and Janakiraman 2003). According to the behavioral explanation managerial overconfidence increases cost stickiness. The intuition is that overconfident managers tend to overestimate future demand and therefore are more likely to retain excess resources when activity levels decline (Banker et al. 2014, Chen, Gores, and Nasev 2013). The agency explanation for cost stickiness has two implications. On one hand, empire building in the sense of maintaining redundant resources to benefit from the prestige of firm size (Jensen and Meckling 1976) will increase cost stickiness (Chen, Lu, and Sougiannis 2012). On the other hand, earnings management in the sense of incentives to meet earnings targets and hence slash redundant resources will reduce cost stickiness (Dierynck, Landsman, and Renders 2012; Kama and Weiss 2013).

While many studies examine determinants of cost stickiness, fewer analyze its implications. One implication of cost stickiness studied by prior literature is its impact on future earnings: Banker and Chen (2006b) show that incorporating asymmetric cost behavior in earnings prediction models outperforms standard approaches. Anderson et al. (2007) document that the common interpretation of an increase in the SG&A ratio as a negative future earnings signal depends on the direction of the change in sales. They show that an increase in SG&A costs in revenue decreasing period sends a positive signal about future performance. This holds in particular for an intended increase (Baumgarten, Bonenkamp, and Homburg 2010). In addition, Weiss (2010) argues that cost stickiness increases earnings volatility. Another sticky cost implication studied by prior literature are

138 As shown in Section 2.2, from theoretical perspective the sources for cost stickiness occurrence are more diverse. Nevertheless, the accounting research literature puts accent on above mentioned three sources. The classification and integration of economic, behavioral, and agency explanations into entire cost stickiness dimensions is illustrated in Figure 2.6.

analyst forecasts: Weiss (2010) documents that analysts' earnings forecasts are less accurate for sticky firms implying that cost stickiness exacerbates the predictability of earnings. Ciftci, Mashruwala, and Weiss (2016) support this finding by documenting that analysts do not fully recognize sticky cost behavior. Focusing on macroeconomic consequences of cost stickiness Rouxelin, Wongsunwai, and Yehuda (2015) find that aggregate cost stickiness predicts lower future unemployment rates four quarters ahead.[139]

A series of papers document the relevance of financial statement information for corporate bankruptcy and firm credit risk. Callen, Livnat, and Segal (2009) find that during 2002 to 2005 CDS premia decrease by 4.5 basis points in response to a 1% increase in earnings. Several recent studies confirm this negative relation between profitability and changes in credit spreads and are overall consistent with the notion that profitable firms have a lower default risk (Das, Hanouna, and Sarin 2009; Easton, Monahan, and Vasvari 2009; Shivakumar, Urcan, Vasvari, and Zhang 2011; Gkougkousi 2014). Further studies focus on accounting-based risk measures. For instance, Chen, Liao, and Chen (2014) find that uncertainty in production efficiency increases bond yield spreads. In addition, Correia, Kang, and Richardson (2015) show that accounting-based (idiosyncratic) measures of asset volatility add to market-based (systematic) measures for the assessment of credit risk. Also accounting information risk is shown to affect credit risk. For example, Kraft (2015) reports that greater rating adjustments to financial statements increase CDS spreads. More generally, better asset reliability decreases credit spreads (Yu 2005; Kim, Kraft and Ryan 2013; Arora, Richardson, and Tuna 2014).

Despite this empirical evidence on the effect of cost stickiness on accounting-based performance measures as well as the documented impact of these measures on corporate credit risk, virtually no previous study examines the direct relation between asymmetric cost behavior and corporate credit spreads. Note that according to prior literature (i) stickiness is positively related to future earnings (Anderson et al. 2007) and earnings volatility (Weiss 2010) and (ii) increasing earnings in turn are shown to decrease credit risk (Callen, Livnat, and Segal 2009) while higher earnings volatility increases credit risk (Correia, Kang, and Richardson 2015). As a consequence, from an empirical perspective, the direction of the direct effect of cost stickiness on credit risk is unclear a priori. On top of these channels, stickiness could affect credit risk through its negative impact on the accuracy of accounting information (Weiss 2010) which itself increases credit risk.

---

139 In Section 2.4.3 I present the details of methodology, data, and the main findings of these research articles.

Based on these considerations I derive the hypotheses from a structural credit model perspective: in short, more cost stickiness will lead to higher earnings volatility, higher accounting information risk, and in some circumstances also to higher future earnings.[140] This translates into higher asset volatility, lower accounting transparency, and higher asset values. The first and second channel will increase firm's default probability and thus credit risk while the third channel eventually reduces credit risk.

Concerning the first channel, I argue that keeping excess resources when current activity levels decline and future activity levels are uncertain can be viewed as an investment in a risky project and therefore stickier firms should have higher credit risk. More specifically, when sales decrease, managers have the choice to either cut resources or maintain unutilized resources. Intuitively, all else equal, managers who decide to keep unutilized resources will accept a larger current earnings decline than managers who adjust resources downwards. Hence, keeping unutilized resources will increase earnings volatility. This link is shown in the model proposed by Weiss (2010). I argue that an increased earnings volatility (e.g. idiosyncratic risk) will increase asset volatility in a similar way as an increased cash flow volatility will increase asset volatility as formally shown by for example Goldstein, Ju, and Leland (2001) and Duffie and Lando (2001).[141] In turn, higher asset volatility will increase default probability as shown in structural models such as Merton (1974). In these models corporate debt is a risk-free bond less a put option on the value of the firm's assets with a strike price at the face value of the firm's debt. If the value of the firm's assets drops below the strike price the firm defaults. Firms with more volatile operating income are more likely to cross the default boundary. Therefore, higher earnings volatility increases credit spreads.

Concerning the second channel, I claim that cost stickiness negatively impacts the precision of accounting information. The intuition is the following: first, cost stickiness increases earnings volatility (Weiss 2010). Second, higher earnings volatility reduces earnings persistence (Dichev and Tang 2009), which is viewed as

---

140 As shown in Chapter 2, cost stickiness can arise from non-economic reasons such as managerial overconfidence, empire building, failure to control costs, etc. In this case I do not expect the value enhancing effect of asymmetric costs.

141 Various studies document empirically the impact of cash flow or earnings volatility on credit risk. For instance, Güntay and Hackbarth (2010), Douglas, Huang, and Vetzal (2014), Molina (2005) show a positive relation of earnings volatility on bond yield spreads and Hann, Heflin, and Subramanayam (2007) on credit ratings. Minton and Schrand (1999) and Douglas, Huang, and Vetzal (2014) provide evidence of a positive link between cash flow volatility and bond yield spreads, and Tang and Yan (2010) confirm the effect on CDS spreads. Pastor and Veronesi (2003) and Wei and Zhang (2006) document that higher volatility of earnings is associated with higher stock returns volatility. Lastly, Campbell and Taksler (2003) and Ericsson, Jacobs, and Oviedo (2009) document a positive link between equity volatility and credit risk.

one dimension of earnings quality (Francis et al. 2005). Hence, I expect that cost stickiness will reduce earnings quality. A lower earnings quality in turn should increase credit spreads. An empirical investigation by Yu (2005), who documents that firms with higher accounting transparency tend to have lower credit spreads, supports this link. From a theory perspective, Duffie and Lando (2001) build an incomplete accounting information model showing that the lack of precise knowledge of a firm's asset value increases default risk and thus credit spreads. While Duffie and Lando's structural credit risk model assumes that accounting reports are unbiased, biased reports should increase credit spreads even further (Shin 2003).[142]

Concerning the third channel, I argue that retaining redundant resources can be viewed as a profitable investment project that may increase future earnings and therefore stickier firms would have lower credit risk. Put differently, rational acting managers engage in active cost management when they consider this to be a value-enhancing strategy. Thus, stickier firms will be associated with higher earnings and asset values. Ceteris paribus, higher asset values push firms further away from the default boundary leading to lower default probabilities within structural credit risk models. Therefore, higher earnings decrease credit spreads.

Assuming that all three channels are effective, the question arises whether the increase in asset value (channel 3) overcompensates the increase in both asset volatility and uncertainty about the asset value (channels 1 and 2). Since especially the link between cost stickiness and earnings seems to be quite weak from an empirical perspective, I do not anticipate channel 3 to dominate channels 1 and 2. I therefore hypothesize that stickier firms have higher credit spreads.

4.3 Data and Methodology

4.3.1 Sample Selection

I use CDS spreads to proxy for credit risk because many prior studies document that CDS spreads are a superior measure of credit risk compared to bond prices or credit ratings.[143] CDS data are obtained from the Markit CDS Composite database, one of

142 According to Shin's disclosure game, disclosed firm values are upward-biased with a bias increasing in decreasing disclosure quality.

143 Ericsson, Jacobs, and Oviedo (2009) show that the majority of CDS spreads is attributable to default risk. Blanco, Brennan, and Marsh (2005) and Zhu (2006) find that the CDS market

the largest providers of CDS data. Markit receives the CDS data from a large sample of banks and aggregates it into a composite number; thereby Markit tests for stale data, outliers, and inconsistencies, ensuring reasonably continuous and accurate price quotations.[144] The investigation spans the period from 2001 to 2011. The CDS data consists of quotes on U.S. dollar denominated CDS on senior unsecured and subordinated debt. To enhance the homogeneity of the sample I follow Callen, Livnat, and Segal (2009) and do not include modified-modified restructuring clauses.[145] To ensure that all financial statement data is available for investors, I merge the sample with Compustat and CRSP requiring that each observation has a CDS premium on the first working day after the SEC filing day (main sample) or 45 days after the fiscal quarter end if the SEC filing date is missing (extended sample). The median of the lag between fiscal quarter end and the date on which the CDS premium is measured equals 40 (44) days in the main (extended) sample. Prior accounting studies measure CDS premia in different ways: a day after the SEC filing day or a day after the preliminary earnings release day (Callen, Livnat, and Segal 2009), a range from 42 to 48 days after the quarter end (Bhat, Callen, and Segal 2014; Kraft 2015) or at the fiscal quarter end (Das, Hanouna, and Sarin 2009).[146] Since credit markets incorporate new information very fast, I consider the SEC filing date as most appropriate to measure the CDS premium minimizing the risk of capturing other information unrelated to the financial statements. Since the SEC filing date is not always available, I repeat the analysis based on the extended sample and show the results in the robustness checks.

---

incorporates changes in credit risk more quickly than the bond market and Acharya and Johnson (2007) document that the CDS market leads the equity market in the price discovery.

144 Evidence for the superiority of Markit among Credit Market Analytics CDS data providers is given by Mayordomo, Peña, and Schwartz (2014) who show that the Markit data set incorporates new information faster than other CDS data sets. For various accounting and finance studies that use the Markit CDS data see e.g., Jorion and Zhang (2007, 2009), Shivakumar et al. (2011), Qiu and Yu (2012), Kim, Kraft, and Ryan (2013), Arora, Richardson, and Tuna (2014).

145 A restructuring clause defines the credit events that trigger settlements. Each restructuring rule has different clauses regarding the maturity and transferability of deliverable obligations. The more flexibility a protection buyer has to deliver a bond, the more valuable the CDS contract. Under the modified-modified restructuring clause the deliverable obligation against the contract has to be limited to those with maturity of 60 months for restructured obligations and 30 months for all other obligations. This is most commonly used in Europe (see Markit 2008, p. 28).

146 Research of equity and bond markets usually constructs the sample with a lag varying between two and six months (see for example Campbell, Chichernea, and Petkevich 2016).

To avoid distortions caused by outliers, I trim the data by deleting the top and bottom 0.5% observations of each continuous variable (Chen and Dixon 1972).[147] The main (extended) sample contains 42,185 (69,310) quarterly CDS spreads of 137 (160) firms.

Table 4.1: Frequency of observations of the main sample

Panel A: Sample breakdown by year

Year	Frequency	Percent
2001	1,335	3.16
2002	2,874	6.81
2003	3,482	8.25
2004	5,696	13.5
2005	6,826	16.18
2006	5,516	13.08
2007	3,090	7.32
2008	2,843	6.74
2009	2,459	5.83
2010	3,293	7.81
2011	4,771	11.31
Total	42,185	100.00

Panel B: Sample breakdown by industry

Industry	Frequency	Percent
Basic Materials	686	1.63
Consumer Goods	6,517	15.45
Consumer Services	7,839	18.58
Financials	14,043	33.29
Health Care	2,173	5.15
Industrials	3,417	8.10
Oil & Gas	2,151	5.10
Technology	2,206	5.23

147 I apply alternative outlier treatments, to which I refer in the robustness checks in Section 4.6.

Table 4.1 continued

Telecommunications	960	2.28
Utilities	2,193	5.20
Total	42,185	100.00

Panel C: Sample breakdown by maturity

Maturity	Frequency	Percent
6-months	2,643	6.27
1-year	4,475	10.61
2-years	4,297	10.19
3-years	4,806	11.39
4-years	2,217	5.26
5-years	5,185	12.29
7-years	4,732	11.22
10-years	4,608	10.92
15-years	3,230	7.66
20-years	3,308	7.84
30-years	2,684	6.36
Total	42,185	100.00

Table 4.1 shows the frequency of observations with respect to year (Panel A), industry (Panel B), and maturity (Panel C) of CDS contracts in the main sample. The industries are classified according to the Industry Classification Benchmark. The sample distribution is comparable to the ones of recent CDS studies by Griffin, Hong, Kim, and Lim (2015) and Chiu, Guan, and Kim (2015) that use the Markit CDS composite data. Most firms are financials, consumer service and consumer goods firms with 5-years being the most represented contracts. The breakdown of the extended sample with respect to year, industry, and maturity shows similar patterns.

4.3.2 Model Specification and Variable Measurement

To estimate the impact of cost stickiness on credit risk, I use OLS regressions with firm and year fixed effects and robust standard errors clustered at the firm level (Petersen 2009):

$$LOG\_CDS_{i,t+1} = \alpha_0 + \alpha_1 STICKY_{i,t} + Firm\ Fixed\ Effects + Year\ Fixed\ Effects + \varepsilon_{i,t+1}. \quad (4.1)$$

with:

$LOG\_CDS_{i,t+1}$ = log of CDS premium in basis points measured on a working day after the SEC filing day of a firm *i*

$STICKY_{i,t}$ = sticky measure on a quarterly basis of firm *i* at quarter end *t*.

Firm fixed effects are included to control for time invariant firm characteristics. In robustness checks I also report firm random effects regressions. In addition, I include year fixed effects to control for factors that affect all firms in a given year.

The main variable in the analysis, STICKY, measures the stickiness of a firm with slightly modified formula of Weiss (2010), originally presented in Section 2.3.2. In detail, I multiply the sticky measure of Weiss (2010) by minus one so that higher values of STICKY imply more stickiness:

$$STICKY_{i,t} = -\left[log\left(\frac{\Delta COST}{\Delta SALE}\right)_{i,\underline{\tau}} - log\left(\frac{\Delta COST}{\Delta SALE}\right)_{i,\overline{\tau}}\right] \quad (4.2)$$

$$with\ \underline{\tau}, \overline{\tau} \in \{t, \dots, t-3\},$$

where $\underline{\tau}$ is the most recent of the last four quarters with a decrease in sales and $\overline{\tau}$ is the most recent of the last four quarters with an increase in sales, $\Delta SALE_{i,t} = SALE_{i,t} - SALE_{i,t-1}$, $\Delta COST_{i,t} = (SALE_{i,t} - EARNINGS_{i,t}) - (SALE_{i,t-1} - EARNINGS_{i,t-1})$, and $EARNINGS$ is income before extraordinary items.

To control for well-known CDS factors, I use the credit spreads determinants that Collin-Dufresne, Goldstein, and Martin (2001) derive from structural models. Callen, Livnat, and Segal (2009), Das, Hanouna, and Sarin (2009), and Ericsson, Jacobs, and Oviedo (2009) implement a similar regression analysis using key variables suggested by economic theory. I follow these studies and extend Eq. 4.1 by adding the following CDS determinants:

$$LOG\_CDS_{i,t+1} = \alpha_0 + \alpha_1 STICKY_{i,t} + \alpha_2 LEV_{i,t} + \alpha_3 RF_t + \alpha_4 VOL_{i,t} + \alpha_5 SENIORITY_{i,t} + \alpha_6 CUMR_{i,t} + \alpha_7 EXR_{i,t} + \alpha_8 SIZE_{i,t} + \alpha_9 ROA_{i,t} + Firm\ Fixed\ Effects \quad (4.3)$$

$$+ Year\ Fixed\ Effects + \varepsilon_{i,t+1}.$$

To estimate Eq. 4.3, I use OLS and cluster standard errors at the firm level.

In the following, I explain the control variables: leverage, risk-free rate, volatility, seniority, restructuring clause, size and profitability. The structural models based on Merton (1974) identify three key determinants of credit spreads: leverage, risk-free rate and asset volatility. I estimate unadjusted leverage (LEV_UA) as total debt divided by market value of assets (computed as market value of equity plus total liabilities) at quarter end. The Merton (1974) framework predicts that a firm defaults when its leverage ratio approaches unity. Therefore, credit spreads should be an increasing function of the firm's leverage.[148] It is likely that cost stickiness affects leverage, the direction of the effect however is unclear and will depend on how cost stickiness affects future cash flows and the discount rate. Since some of the variation in stickiness may explain some of the variation in leverage, as leverage control variable I use the variation in leverage that is not explained by stickiness. Hence, the proxy for leverage (LEV) is the error term from the following regression $LEV\_UA_{i,t} = \alpha_0 + \alpha_1 STICKY_{i,t} + \text{year fixed effects} + \varepsilon_{i,t}$.

The risk-free rate (RF) is measured as the one-year Treasury-bill rate. The risk-free rate is an important determinant of credit risk in structural models because it impacts the value of the put option. Economically, high interest rates are usually related to economic upturns. Hence, I expect that the risk-free rate reduces credit spreads.[149]

Asset volatility is another key determinant of the value of default-sensitive securities. Higher volatility increases the value of the put option resulting in higher credit spreads. I measure the volatility of equity as the standard deviation of daily returns during the firm's current fiscal quarter (VOL_UA). The standard deviation of returns is a commonly employed proxy and it has been empirically shown to influence credit risk (Campbell and Taksler 2003; Ericsson, Jacobs, and Oviedo 2009). To eliminate the volatility that is driven by cost stickiness I use the error terms from the following regression $VOL\_UA_{i,t} = \alpha_0 + \alpha_1 STICKY_{i,t} + \text{year fixed effects} + \varepsilon_{i,t}$ as proxy for asset volatility (VOL). This measure should contain idiosyncratic as well as systematic volatility unrelated to stickiness. I further control for seniority following Das, Hanouna, and Sarin (2009). The indicator

148 See for example Zhang, Zhou, and Zhu (2009), Chen, Tseng, and Hsieh (2015) for empirical evidence.

149 Studies that support this expectation are Collin-Dufresne, Goldstein, and Martin (2001), Callen, Livnat, and Segal (2009) and Das, Hanouna, and Sarin (2009).

variable SENIORITY is equal to one (zero) if the credit default swap refers to senior unsecured (subordinated) debt and equals zero otherwise.

To control for the type of restructuring clause, I use dummies. Restructuring clauses define credit events, which trigger settlement. The International Swaps and Derivative Association provides four choices under restructuring as a credit event: full restructuring, modified restructuring, modified-modified restructuring, and no restructuring. Each restructuring rule has different clauses regarding the maturity and transferability of deliverable obligations.[150] Packer and Zhu (2005) and Berndt, Jarrow, and Kang (2007) confirm the relevance of the restructuring clauses on CDS premia. To denote full restructuring, I use the indicator variable CUMR, the variable EXR represents no restructuring, and the modified restructuring clause is captured by the intercept. The broader the range of the credit event and/or the fewer the restrictions on the settlement obligations, the more valuable is the CDS protection. Therefore, I expect the CDS spreads to be higher in the case of a full restructuring clause and lower in the case of no restructuring clause.

To control for accounting transparency which is inversely related to credit risk (Duffie and Lando 2001), I follow Callen, Livnat, and Segal (2009) and use firm size (SIZE_UA) defined as the logarithm of market value of equity. Since I expect that higher cost stickiness increases accounting information risk and reduces accounting transparency (channel 2), I eliminate the effect of accounting transparency caused by cost stickiness and measure SIZE as the error term from the following regression $SIZE\_UA_{i,t} = \alpha_0 + \alpha_1 STICKY_{i,t} + \text{year fixed effects} + \varepsilon_{i,t}$.

Following Chiu, Guan, and Kim (2015) I control for profitability that is negatively related to credit risk as documented by prior studies (Benkert 2004; Das, Hanouna, and Sarin 2009; Callen, Livnat, and Segal 2009). I calculate the unadjusted return on assets (ROA_UA) as the quarterly net income before extraordinary items divided by the prior period total assets.[151] Since cost stickiness influences earnings, which in turn will have an effect on credit risk, I eliminate the variation in profitability that is induced by cost stickiness with the following regression $ROA\_UA_{i,t} = \alpha_0 + \alpha_1 STICKY_{i,t} + \text{year fixed effects} + \varepsilon_{i,t}$ and use the error term as proxy for profitability (ROA).

In addition to the analysis based on 5-year CDS contracts, I also estimate the effect of cost stickiness on credit risk using CDS contracts with all available maturities. To control for CDS maturity, I use indicator variables D_k denoting CDS maturities of

150 See Packer and Zhu (2005) for detailed discussions on the contractual terms regarding restructuring.

151 When I calculate profitability as net income scaled by the sum of firm market equity and total liabilities, the results do not change qualitatively.

k years $k \in I = \{1, 2, 3, 4, 5, 7, 10, 15, 20, 30\}$, where CDS contracts of 6-months are captured by the intercept. Prior research documents positive association between maturity and CDS premia (e.g., Callen, Livnat, and Segal 2009; Das, Hanouna, and Sarin 2009; and Douglas, Huarng, and Vetzal 2014). From a theoretical perspective, however, the direction of the effect is unclear ex-ante. Eq. 4.4 extends Eq. 4.3 by including the maturity dummies:

$$\begin{aligned} LOG\_CDS_{i,t+1} = {} & \alpha_0 + \alpha_1 STICKY_{i,t} + \alpha_2 LEV_{i,t} + \alpha_3 RF_t \\ & + \alpha_4 VOL_{i,t} + \alpha_5 SENIORITY_{i,t} + \alpha_6 CUMR_{i,t} \\ & + \alpha_7 EXR_{i,t} + \alpha_8 SIZE_{i,t} + \alpha_9 ROA_{i,t} \\ & + \sum_{k \in I} \alpha_{10+k} D\_k_{i,t} + Firm\ Fixed\ Effects \\ & + Year\ Fixed\ Effects + \varepsilon_{i,t+1}. \end{aligned} \quad 4.4$$

4.4 Empirical Results

4.4.1 Descriptive Statistics

Table 4.2 presents descriptive statistics of the main sample. The sample firms are relatively large; the average (median) market value is \$24.83 (\$8.36) billion. The average (median) log of CDS premium one working day after the SEC filing day (LOG_CDS) is equal to 4.82 (4.88) with a standard deviation of 1.25, representing an average (median) premium of 255.29 (131.99) basis points. Figure 4.2 demonstrates the rationale for using the logarithm of CDS spreads. While the left-hand graph shows a skewed distribution of CDS spreads, the right-hand graph illustrates that the sample of CDS spreads is closer to normal distribution after taking the logarithm.

Figure 4.2: Distribution of CDS spreads before and after taking the logarithm

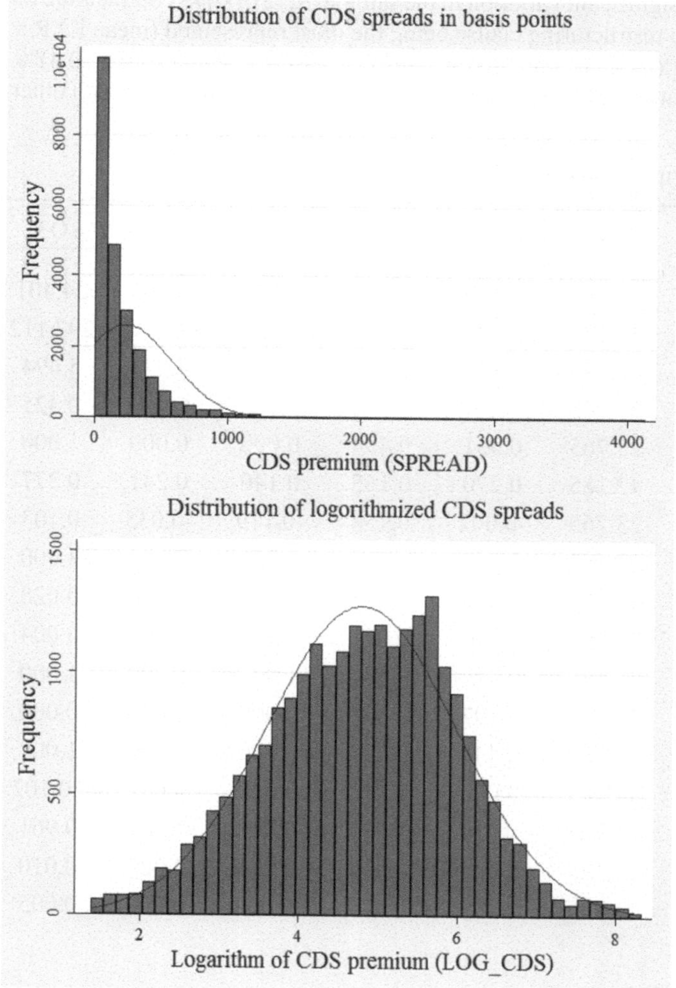

The sticky variable has a mean (median) value equal to -0.14 (-0.04). 45% of the sample firms exhibit positive values of the cost stickiness measure, which approximately corresponds to the previous studies analyzing asymmetric cost behavior.[152] The unadjusted leverage is on average equal to 0.27 and has

[152] For example Weiss (2010) reports 53.2% of firms with sticky costs.

considerable variation of 0.17. The standard deviation of equity returns and the risk-free rate show also significant variation in the sample. 82% of CDS contracts are on senior debt, with no restructuring clause being the most represented (mean EXR = 44%). The average (median) unadjusted return on assets is equal to 0.5 (0.4)%. Overall, the distributions of key variables in my sample are comparable with other CDS studies.

Table 4.2: Descriptive statistics of the main sample

Variable	N	Mean	SD	Q1	Median	Q3
MV	42,185	24,826	42,240	3,128	8,363	24,401
SPREAD	42,185	255.294	380.060	52.400	131.992	297.112
LOG_CDS	42,185	4.820	1.247	3.959	4.883	5.694
STICKY	23,765	-0.138	1.158	-0.651	-0.042	0.425
D_STICKY	23,765	0.451	0.498	0.000	0.000	1.000
LEV_UA	42,185	0.270	0.165	0.140	0.241	0.377
LEV	23,765	-0.002	0.158	-0.119	-0.035	0.103
RF	42,185	2.408	1.729	0.700	2.080	3.900
VOL_UA	42,185	0.024	0.015	0.014	0.020	0.028
VOL	23,765	-0.001	0.011	-0.008	-0.003	0.004
SENIORITY	42,185	0.817	0.386	1.000	1.000	1.000
CUMR	42,185	0.197	0.398	0.000	0.000	0.000
EXR	42,185	0.441	0.497	0.000	0.000	1.000
SIZE_UA	42,185	9.092	1.475	8.048	9.032	10.102
SIZE	23,765	0.010	1.433	-1.044	-0.030	0.961
ROA_UA	42,185	0.005	0.015	0.001	0.004	0.010
ROA	23,765	0.001	0.012	-0.004	0.000	0.005

Variable Definitions:

MV	Market value (in $MM) of equity calculated as close price (PRCCQ) multiplied by common shares outstanding (CSHOQ) at the end of the fiscal quarter;
SPREAD	CDS spread in basis points measured on a working day after the SEC filing day;
LOG_CDS	Log of CDS premium in basis points measured on a working day after

	the SEC filing day;
STICKY	Sticky measure on a quarterly basis. It is calculated as: $STICKY_{i,t} = -[\log(\Delta COST/\Delta SALE)_{i,\underline{\tau}} - \log(\Delta COST/\Delta SALE)_{i,\overline{\tau}}]$, with $\underline{\tau}, \overline{\tau} \in \{t,..,t-3\}$; $\underline{\tau}$ is the most recent of the last four quarters with a decrease in sales and $\overline{\tau}$ is most recent of the last four quarters with an increase in sales. COST = sales (SALEQ) – earnings (IBQ);
D_STICKY	An indicator variable equal to 1 if STICKY > 0 and 0 otherwise;
LEV_UA	Leverage, computed as long term debt (DLTTQ) scaled by the value of assets (market value of equity (PRCCQ*CSHOQ)+book value of total liabilities (LTQ));
LEV	Residuals from the following cross-sectional regression: $\text{LEV\_UA}_{i,t} = \alpha_0 + \alpha_1 \text{STICKY}_{i,t} + \text{year fixed effects} + \varepsilon_{i,t}$;
RF	One-year T-Bill rate;
VOL_UA	Standard deviation of daily returns (RET) during the firm's current fiscal quarter;
VOL	Residuals from the following cross-sectional regression: $\text{VOL\_UA}_{i,t} = \alpha_0 + \alpha_1 \text{STICKY}_{i,t} + \text{year fixed effects} + \varepsilon_{i,t}$;
SENIORITY	An indicator variable equal to 1 if the underlying CDS contract is senior and 0 otherwise;
CUMR	An indicator variable equal to 1 if the CDS contract has a full restructuring clause and 0 otherwise;
EXR	An indicator variable equal to 1 if the CDS contract has no restructuring clause and 0 otherwise;
SIZE_UA	Log of market value of equity;
SIZE	Residuals from the following cross-sectional regression: $\text{SIZE\_UA}_{i,t} = \alpha_0 + \alpha_1 \text{STICKY}_{i,t} + \text{year fixed effects} + \varepsilon_{i,t}$;
ROA_UA	The return on assets, calculated as quarterly income before extraordinary items (IBQ) scaled by total assets (ATQ) in the previous period;
ROA	Residuals from the following cross-sectional regression: $\text{ROA\_UA}_{i,t} = \alpha_0 + \alpha_1 \text{STICKY}_{i,t} + \text{year fixed effects} + \varepsilon_{i,t}$.

The descriptive statistics of the extended sample are similar to the sample discussed above. Unreported Variance Inflation Factors indicate that the regression models do not suffer from multicollinearity.

4.4.2 Main Results

Table 4.3 presents results of the effect of cost stickiness on credit risk based on the main sample. Panel A of Table 4.3 shows the results for 5-year CDS contracts, which are the most common and the most liquid CDS contracts. Column 1 presents the result for Eq. 4.1 where credit spreads are regressed on cost stickiness, firm and year fixed effects without controls. The coefficient of STICKY is as expected positive (coefficient = 0.0430) and significant at the 5% level. This result suggests that the increase in asset volatility and higher accounting information risk (channels 1 and 2) dominate a potential increase in asset value (channel 3), which is consistent with my hypothesis that cost stickiness increases credit spreads.

Table 4.3: Regression results based on the main sample

Panel A: Based on the sample covering only 5-year CDS contracts

Variable	Exp. sign	LOG_CDS (1)	LOG_CDS (2)
STICKY	+	0.0430**	0.0691***
		(2.21)	(4.55)
LEV	+		0.8534*
			(1.91)
RF	-		-0.1272***
			(-3.44)
VOL	+		14.7584***
			(6.49)
SENIORITY	-		-0.2442***
			(-7.53)
CUMR	+		0.0521***
			(4.44)
EXR	-		-0.0469***
			(-2.98)
SIZE	-		-0.4803***
			(-5.56)
ROA	-		0.8698
			(0.37)
Constant	+/-	4.7532***	4.8907***
		(31.20)	(28.21)
N		2,906	2,906
Number of firms		130	130
Firm FE		YES	YES
Year FE		YES	YES
Adjusted R^2		0.3540	0.5651

Panel B: Based on subsamples of CDS contracts with different maturities

Variable	Exp. sign	1-year	2-years	3-years	7-years	10-years
STICKY	+	0.0939***	0.0823***	0.0743***	0.0546***	0.0521***
		(4.22)	(4.55)	(4.28)	(3.80)	(3.88)
Controls	+/-	YES	YES	YES	YES	YES
N		2,524	2,410	2,680	2,648	2,581
Number of firms		125	120	128	126	125
Firm FE		YES	YES	YES	YES	YES
Year FE		YES	YES	YES	YES	YES
Adjusted R^2		0.5710	0.5944	0.5801	0.5527	0.5268

Panel C: Based on a sample covering CDS contracts of all maturities

Variable	Exp. sign	LOG_CDS
STICKY	+	0.0696***
		(4.77)
LEV	+	0.6951
		(1.51)
RF	-	-0.1476***
		(-3.70)
VOL	+	15.5385***
		(6.31)
SENIORITY	-	-0.2346***
		(-7.18)
CUMR	+	0.0361**
		(2.45)
EXR	-	-0.0507***
		(-2.75)

Table 4.3 continued

SIZE	-	-0.5176***
		(-6.04)
ROA	-	1.0852
		(0.50)
D_1	+/-	0.2468***
		(10.57)
D_2	+/-	0.4954***
		(17.68)
D_3	+/-	0.7054***
		(23.24)
D_4	+/-	0.8923***
		(28.06)
D_5	+/-	0.9721***
		(28.55)
D_7	+/-	1.0622***
		(28.68)
D_10	+/-	1.1517***
		(29.06)
D_15	+/-	1.2106***
		(28.03)
D_20	+/-	1.2342***
		(27.58)
D_30	+/-	1.2542***
		(27.09)
Constant	+/-	-0.5917***
		(-3.24)
N		23,765
Number of firms		130
Firm FE		YES
Year FE		YES

Table 4.3 continued

Adjusted R^2	0.6072

Table 4.3 shows the panel data regression results of the effect of cost stickiness on credit risk based on the main sample. Panel A presents the results for 5-year CDS contracts. Column 1 shows the result for Eq. 4.1 where credit spreads are regressed on cost stickiness, firm and year fixed effects without controls. Column 2 shows the result for the model, which augments the Column 1 with controls.

Panel B shows the results for subsamples that cover different CDS maturities based on the following regression:

$$LOG\_CDS_{i,t+1} = \alpha_0 + \alpha_1 STICKY_{i,t} + \alpha_2 LEV_{i,t} + \alpha_3 RF_t + \alpha_4 VOL_{i,t} + \alpha_5 SENIORITY_{i,t} + \alpha_6 CUMR_{i,t} + \alpha_7 EXR_{i,t} + \alpha_8 SIZE_{i,t} + \alpha_9 ROA_{i,t} + Firm\ Fixed\ Effects + Year\ Fixed\ Effects + \varepsilon_{i,t+1}.$$

Panel C presents the results of the effect of cost stickiness on credit spreads based on the sample covering all available contracts with different maturities.

*(**, ***) Denotes significance at the 10% (5%, 1%) level (two-tailed). All continuous variables are trimmed at the 0.5%. The t-statistics in parentheses are calculated using robust standard errors clustered by the firm. In this table, every given firm is represented as many times as CDS spreads are available for that company. The coefficients of firm and year are suppressed. The dependent variable is log of CDS premium one working day after the SEC filing. The independent variables are STICKY and control variables as defined in Table 4.2.

Column 2 shows the result for Eq. 4.3 which augments Eq. 4.1 with controls. When control variables are included, the coefficient of STICKY rises to 0.0691 and is statistical significant at the 1% level. This suggests that the increase of cost stickiness by one unit leads to 7.15% (= exp (0.0691)-1) higher CDS spreads. To provide a more intuitive interpretation of the results, I standardize all continuous independent variables and measure the dependent variable in basis points.[153] The STICKY coefficient equals 26.78 and is statistically significant at the 1% level. This implies that a one standard deviation increase of cost stickiness leads to a 27 basis points increase in CDS spreads on average.[154]

Regarding the control variables, consistent with prior literature I find that higher levered firms exhibit higher credit spreads. The coefficient of LEV is positive and statistically significant. The effects of SENIORITY, RF and SIZE are negative and highly significant consistent with prior work. The magnitude of the effect of asset

153 Standardization means subtracting the average value of a variable and divided by its' standard deviation (see Wooldridge 2013, p. 182).

154 The results are reported in Appendix 4.

volatility is as expected positive and highly significant. While the full restructuring clause (CUMR) increases, no restructuring clause (EXR) reduces CDS premia also as predicted. The profitability variable (ROA) is insignificant and remains insignificant but has the expected sign if I exclude the STICKY variable and use the unadjusted standard deviation of returns (VOL_UA), size (SIZE_UA), and leverage (LEV_UA) instead of the stickiness adjusted return volatility (VOL), size (SIZE), and leverage (LEV) respectively.[155]

Panel B of Table 4.3 shows the effect of cost stickiness on credit risk for additional subsamples that cover different CDS maturities. The coefficient of STICKY is positive and highly statistically significant across all maturities.[156] Moreover, the stickiness effect is more pronounced for short-term spreads and decreases with maturity, consistent with structural credit model implications that changes in volatility have less impact on credit spreads for longer maturities.

Panel C of Table 4.3 presents the results based on the sample pooled over all maturities (Eq. 4.4). Now, the sample size increases to 23,765 observations. Again, I find clear evidence that cost stickiness is positively related to credit risk. The effect holds regardless of whether I control for well-known credit risk determinants or omit controls. Compared to the main sample covering 5-year CDS contracts (Panel A) the key coefficients of interest remain unchanged, in terms of both magnitude and statistical significance. Further, consistent with prior work (e.g., Griffin et al. 2015) I also find that CDS spreads increase in CDS maturity.

4.4.3 Cross-Sectional Variation

In the following I study the effect of cost stickiness on credit risk by analyzing the cross-sectional variation that arises from differences in firms' favorable environment.[157]

Firms that operate under more favorable conditions are able to make more efficient cost decisions, reducing the cost stickiness and operating risk which in turn results in lower CDS premia. Therefore I expect the association between cost stickiness and credit risk to be lower for firms with a favorable environment. To test this prediction

155 The expected negative sign for profitability is further observed in the specification with standardized variables (Table A.1) as well as various robustness checks (Table 4.8, Table 4.9, Table 4.10).

156 I report the results only for the most frequent contracts except for the 5-year CDS already presented in Panel A.

157 The analysis in this section is motivated by Chen, Kacperczyk, and Ortiz-Molina (2011), who demonstrate that labor unions increase firms' costs of equity by decreasing firms' operating flexibility.

I interact the STICKY variable with one of the two proxies for favorable conditions (COND) and rerun the Eq. 4.3 by adding the interaction term and the COND variable.

$$
\begin{aligned}
LOG\_CDS_{i,t+1} = \; & \alpha_0 + \alpha_1 STICKY_{i,t} + \alpha_2 COND_{i,t} \\
& + \alpha_3 STICKY_{i,t} \times COND_{i,t} + \alpha_4 LEV_{i,t} \\
& + \alpha_5 RF_t + \alpha_6 VOL_{i,t} + \alpha_7 SENIORITY_{i,t} \\
& + \alpha_8 CUMR_{i,t} + \alpha_9 EXR_{i,t} + \alpha_{10} SIZE_{i,t} \\
& + \alpha_{11} ROA_{i,t} + Firm\ Fixed\ Effects \\
& + Year\ Fixed\ Effects + \varepsilon_{i,t+1}.
\end{aligned} \qquad 4.5
$$

The first measure of favorable conditions is RTW (right-to-work laws), equal to 1 if the firm is headquartered in a state that passed a right-to-work law as of time t. RTW laws are present in 26 states of the US and are aimed at limiting the power of labor unions. In particular, the RTW laws prohibit agreements between employers and labor unions that presume membership or any payment as a condition of employment. As a consequence, the employees are not protected by union contracts, thus reducing firms' costs of adjustment in sales decline periods and which hence implies a negative coefficient of $STICKY \times RTW$.

The second proxy for favorable conditions is REPUBLICAN, an indicator variable equal to 1, if the firm is headquartered in a state under the influence of the Republican Party. The state is defined as Republican if the Republican Party gained the majority of electoral votes in the most recent presidential election.[158] The idea is that states under Republican influence are assumed to be more employer friendly in contrast to Democratic states which are historically more associated with labor unions. Hence, I expect a negative coefficient of $STICKY \times REPUBLICAN$. The results are reported in Table 4.4.

158 The data is obtained from http://uselectionatlas.org/RESULTS/.

Table 4.4: The effect of favorable conditions

Variable	Exp. sign	LOG_CDS (1)	LOG_CDS (2)
STICKY	+	0.0852***	0.1151***
		(4.26)	(6.17)
RTW	+/-	0.2593	
		(0.79)	
STICKY× *RTW*	-	-0.0521*	
		(-1.78)	
REPUBLICAN	+/-		0.1423
			(1.11)
STICKY×REPUBLICAN	-		-0.1031***
			(-3.66)
LEV	+	0.8534*	0.8059*
		(1.88)	(1.74)
RF	-	-0.1267***	-0.1427***
		(-3.44)	(-3.73)
VOL	+	14.9567***	15.2133***
		(6.55)	(6.44)
SENIORITY	-	-0.2449***	-0.2566***
		(-7.58)	(-7.36)
CUMR	+	0.0520***	0.0511***
		(4.46)	(4.26)
EXR	-	-0.0471***	-0.0443***
		(-3.02)	(-2.73)
SIZE	-	-0.4815***	-0.4720***
		(-5.73)	(-5.47)
ROA	-	0.9529	1.3616
		(0.40)	(0.56)

Table 4.4 continued

Constant	+/-	4.8115***	4.8978***
		(24.66)	(26.28)
N		2,906	2,657
Number of firms		130	115
Firm FE		YES	YES
Year FE		YES	YES
Adjusted R^2		0.5677	0.5720

Table 4.4 shows the panel data regression results for cross-sectional variation in cost stickiness premium. Panel A presents the results for the effect of favorable conditions proxied by RTW (Column 1) or REPUBLICAN (Column 2). *(**, ***) Denotes significance at the 10% (5%, 1%) level (two-tailed). All continuous variables are trimmed at the 0.5%. The t-statistics in parentheses are calculated using robust standard errors clustered by the firm. In this table, every given firm is represented as many times as CDS spreads are available for that company. The coefficients of firm and year are suppressed. The dependent variable is log of CDS premium one working day after the SEC filing. RTW is an indicator variable equal to 1 if the firm is headquartered in the state passed right-to-work law as of time t and 0 otherwise. STICKY× RTW is the interaction term of STICKY and RTW. REPUBLICAN is an indicator variable equal to 1 if the firm is headquartered in the state where the Republican Party gained the majority of electoral votes in the most recent presidential election and 0 otherwise. STICKY×REPUBLICAN is the interaction term of STICKY and REPUBLICAN. All other variables as defined in Table 4.2.

Consistent with the prediction, the coefficients on the interaction terms $STICKY \times RTW$ and $STICKY \times REPUBLICAN$ are negative and statistically significant. The association between cost stickiness and credit risk is weaker when a firm operates in a more favorable environment: in states with RTW laws and Republican influence. This result also provides evidence for the 3rd channel: firms that have the flexibility to cut costs are more likely to avoid an inefficient high level of cost stickiness inducing lower future earnings.

4.5 Addressing Endogeneity Concerns

Reverse causality and omitted correlated variables could potentially bias my results. One could argue that if riskier firms have incentives to become stickier the causality is reversed. I believe this is unlikely and that riskier firms probably have more incentives to cut instead to keep excess costs because by cutting excess resources they can reduce their operating risk. This notion is consistent with Anderson, Banker, and Janakiraman (2003) who report that firms in more uncertain demand environments measured as higher past sales volatility are less sticky. Nonetheless, to alleviate potential reverse causality concerns, I lag the STICKY variable and re-estimate Eqs. 4.1, 4.3, and 4.4. The results reported in Table 4.5 show that the coefficient of lagged STICKY is positive and highly statistical significant supporting my argument that the causality runs from stickiness to credit spreads and not the other way around.

To address correlated omitted variables, I include firm fixed effects in the main specification in Table 4.3. Firm fixed effects control for unobservable time invariant firm characteristics. Yet, I acknowledge that I cannot control for unobservable time varying firm factors. In a similar way, year fixed effects, which are also included in the main model (Table 4.3) control for market wide factors that affect all firms in the same year.

Table 4.5: Regression results lagging the main independent variable STICKY for the sample covering 5-year CDS contracts and all maturities

		LOG_CDS			
		5-years		all maturities	
Variable	Exp. sign	(1)	(2)	(3)	(4)
L_STICKY	+	0.0429***	0.0310***	0.0405**	0.0329***
		(2.78)	(2.65)	(2.37)	(2.93)
LEV	+		1.1947***		1.0594**
			(2.69)		(2.23)
RF	-		-0.1312***		-0.1562***
			(-3.16)		(-3.44)
VOL	+		15.6872***		16.0016***
			(6.28)		(5.86)
SENIORITY	-		-0.2311***		-0.2205***
			(-6.83)		(-6.44)

Table 4.5 continued

CUMR	+	0.0465***	0.0316*
		(3.68)	(1.96)
EXR	-	-0.0496***	-0.0496**
		(-2.97)	(-2.56)
SIZE	-	-0.4710***	-0.5197***
		(-5.07)	(-5.40)
ROA	-	2.9459	3.3014
		(1.19)	(1.32)
D_1	+/-		0.2344***
			(9.39)
D_2	+/-		0.4883***
			(16.08)
D_3	+/-		0.7048***
			(21.06)
D_4	+/-		0.8957***
			(24.47)
D_5	+/-		0.9845***
			(25.37)
D_7	+/-		1.0766***
			(24.70)
D_10	+/-		1.1655***
			(25.09)
D_15	+/-		1.2269***
			(24.44)
D_20	+/-		1.2515***
			(24.45)
D_30	+/-		1.2671***
			(23.89)

Table 4.5 continued

Constant	+/-	4.7624***	4.9158***	4.6128***	-0.5696***
		(30.15)	(29.78)	(27.90)	(-3.17)
N		2,965	2,318	24,272	19,015
Number of firms		132	122	132	122
Firm FE		YES	YES	YES	YES
Year FE		YES	YES	YES	YES
Adjusted R^2		0.3412	0.5734	0.2221	0.6175

Table 4.5 presents the regression results for the lagged STICKY variable. Columns 1 and 2 show the results based on the sample covering only 5-year CDS contracts. Columns 3 and 4 present the results based on the sample covering all available contract with different maturities. *(**, ***) Denotes significance at the 10% (5%, 1%) level (two-tailed). All continuous variables are trimmed at the 0.5%. The t-statistics in parentheses are calculated using robust standard errors clustered by the firm. In this table, every given firm is represented as many times as CDS spreads are available for that company. The coefficients of firm and year are suppressed.

The dependent variable is log of CDS premium one working day after the SEC filing. The independent variables are L_STICKY and control variables as defined in Table 4.2.

4.6 Robustness Checks

Extended Sample

In the main specification, I use the CDS premium a day after the SEC filing date. When I add observations where CDS premia are measured 45 days after the fiscal quarter end if the SEC filing date is missing, the sample size covering 5-year (all maturities) CDS contracts almost doubles, rising from 2,906 (23,765) to 5,219 (42,468). The results including firm fixed or firm random effects[159] are presented in Table 4.6 Panel A (B) for the 5-year (6-months to 30-years) CDS contracts. The effect of cost stickiness on credit risk remains almost unchanged and is highly statistically significant at the 1% level in the case of 5-year CDS contracts as well as in the sample with all maturities.

159 See Callen, Livnat, and Segal (2009, p. 1368) and Das, Hanouna, and Sarin (2009, p. 729) for the discussion of firm fixed versus random effects.

Table 4.6: Regression results based on the extended sample

Panel A: Based on the sample covering 5-year CDS contracts

		LOG_CDS	
Variable	Exp. sign	(1)	(2)
STICKY	+	0.0693***	0.0701***
		(5.43)	(5.78)
LEV	+	0.9026**	1.0766***
		(2.59)	(3.55)
RF	-	-0.1519***	-0.1480***
		(-7.13)	(-7.00)
VOL	+	15.0546***	15.6577***
		(7.43)	(8.25)
SENIORITY	-	-0.2377***	-0.2322***
		(-8.50)	(-8.37)
CUMR	+	0.0451***	0.0458***
		(3.78)	(3.86)
EXR	-	-0.0664***	-0.0592***
		(-4.43)	(-3.87)
SIZE	-	-0.4018***	-0.4022***
		(-5.05)	(-7.23)
ROA	-	-0.9519	-0.9434
		(-0.68)	(-0.68)
Constant	+/-	5.1923***	5.1985***
		(42.18)	(43.28)
N		5,219	5,219
Number of firms		153	153
Firm FE		YES	NO
Year FE		YES	YES
Adjusted R^2		0.5761	0.6555

Panel B: Based on a sample covering CDS contracts of all maturities

Variable	Exp. sign	LOG_CDS (1)	LOG_CDS (2)
STICKY	+	0.0660***	0.0660***
		(4.99)	(5.06)
LEV	+	0.9425**	0.9803***
		(2.45)	(2.63)
RF	-	-0.1698***	-0.1693***
		(-7.53)	(-7.52)
VOL	+	16.4169***	16.5727***
		(7.58)	(7.82)
SENIORITY	-	-0.2321***	-0.2306***
		(-7.73)	(-7.69)
CUMR	+	0.0355**	0.0356**
		(2.55)	(2.56)
EXR	-	-0.0651***	-0.0638***
		(-3.72)	(-3.64)
SIZE	-	-0.4342***	-0.4305***
		(-5.15)	(-5.56)
ROA	-	-0.8834	-0.9013
		(-0.65)	(-0.67)
D_1	+/-	0.2842***	0.2840***
		(13.86)	(13.84)
D_2	+/-	0.5509***	0.5507***
		(24.29)	(24.26)
D_3	+/-	0.7751***	0.7747***
		(31.64)	(31.60)
D_4	+/-	0.9599***	0.9596***
		(36.30)	(36.26)

Table 4.6 continued

D_5	+/-	1.0502***	1.0495***
		(37.71)	(37.63)
D_7	+/-	1.1473***	1.1470***
		(37.06)	(37.01)
D_10	+/-	1.2427***	1.2424***
		(37.09)	(37.04)
D_15	+/-	1.2907***	1.2906***
		(35.81)	(35.81)
D_20	+/-	1.3248***	1.3246***
		(35.32)	(35.32)
D_30	+/-	1.3530***	1.3528***
		(33.27)	(33.27)
Constant	+/-	4.2306***	4.2466***
		(32.34)	(29.75)
N		42,468	42,468
Number of firms		153	153
Firm FE		YES	NO
Year FE		YES	YES
Adjusted R^2		0.6277	0.6452

Table 4.6 presents results the of the effect of cost stickiness on credit risk based on the extended sample, i.e., the dependent variable is log of CDS premium (LOG_CDS) one working day after the SEC filing or 45 days after the financial quarter end if the SEC filing date is missing. Panel A shows the results for 5-year CDS contracts.

Panel B shows the results for all available CDS contracts with different maturities.

*(**, ***) Denotes significance at the 10% (5%, 1%) level (two-tailed). All continuous variables are trimmed at the 0.5%. The t-statistics in parentheses are calculated using robust standard errors clustered by the firm. In this table, every given firm is represented as many times as CDS spreads are available for that company. The coefficients of firm and year are suppressed. The dependent variable is log of CDS premium (LOG_CDS) one working day after the SEC filing or 45 days after the financial quarter end if the SEC filing date is missing. The independent variables are STICKY and control as defined in Table 4.2.

Firm Fixed Effects versus Firm Random Effects

I use firm fixed effects as the main specification to rule out that my findings are driven by time-invariant unobserved individual effects that are correlated with the independent variables. Here I show results for firm random effects that assume that the unobserved heterogeneity is uncorrelated with the regressors.

The evidence in Table 4.7 supports my hypothesis that cost stickiness leads to higher credit spreads. Columns 1 and 2 show that the results remain comparable to the main findings presented in Table 4.3, Panel A, Columns 1 and 2. The coefficients of the control variables and their significance also do not change considerably compared to the main results.

Table 4.7: Robustness based on firm random effects for the sample covering 5-year CDS contracts

Variable	Exp. sign	LOG_CDS (1)	LOG_CDS (2)
STICKY	+	0.0440**	0.0679***
		(2.27)	(4.59)
LEV	+		1.2334***
			(3.67)
RF	-		-0.1180***
			(-3.13)
VOL	+		16.0199***
			(7.66)
SENIORITY	-		-0.2353***
			(-7.28)
CUMR	+		0.0561***
			(4.62)
EXR	-		-0.0379**
			(-2.34)
SIZE	-		-0.4268***
			(-8.11)
ROA	-		0.1894
			(0.08)

Table 4.7 continued

Constant	+/-	4.9161***	4.9139***
		(30.21)	(28.63)
N		2,906	2,906
Number of firms		130	130
Firm FE		NO	NO
Year FE		YES	YES
Adjusted R^2		0.1214	0.6598

Table 4.7 presents results of the effect of cost stickiness on 5–year CDS spreads using firm random effects. The dependent variable is log of CDS premium one working day after the SEC filing. Column 1 shows the results for the regression of credit spreads on cost stickiness, firm random and year fixed effects without controls. Column 2 shows the results for the model, which augments the Column 1 with controls. *(**, ***) Denotes significance at the 10% (5%, 1%) level (two-tailed). All continuous variables are trimmed at the 0.5%. The t-statistics in parentheses are calculated using robust standard errors clustered by the firm. In this table, every given firm is represented as many times as CDS spreads are available for that company. The coefficients of year are suppressed. The independent variables are STICKY and control variables as defined in Table 4.2.

Industry Effects

Next, I check how the results change if instead of firm fixed effects, I use industry fixed effects in the firm random effects specification. Industry fixed effects help rule out that cost stickiness is associated with credit risk only because sticky firms happen to be overrepresented in industries with higher credit risk. Following Gehde-Trapp, Gündüz, and Nasev (2015) I construct industry dummies, where the industry is defined according to the Industry Classification Benchmark provided by Markit. Table 4.8 presents the results, which are comparable to the main results.

Table 4.8: Robustness based on industry fixed effects for the sample covering 5-year CDS contracts

Variable	Exp. sign	LOG_CDS (1)	LOG_CDS (2)
STICKY	+	0.0425**	0.0664***
		(2.21)	(4.49)
LEV	+		1.2499***
			(3.82)
RF	-		-0.1199***
			(-3.15)
VOL	+		16.3227***
			(7.81)
SENIORITY	-		-0.2350***
			(-7.29)
CUMR	+		0.0559***
			(4.60)
EXR	-		-0.0389**
			(-2.42)
SIZE	-		-0.3874***
			(-6.87)
ROA	-		-0.5435
			(-0.24)
Constant	+/-	5.0883***	5.1405***
		(19.25)	(13.79)
N		2,906	2,906
Number of firms		130	130
Firm FE		NO	NO
Year FE		YES	YES
Industry FE		YES	YES
Adjusted R^2		0.4513	0.6943

Table 4.8 continued

Table 4.8 presents results of the effect of cost stickiness on 5–year CDS spreads using firm random and year and industry fixed effects. The dependent variable is log of CDS premium one working day after the SEC filing.

Column 1 shows the results for the regression of credit spreads on cost stickiness, firm random, year and industry fixed effects without controls. Column 2 shows the results for the model, which augments the Column 1 with controls. *(**, ***) Denotes significance at the 10% (5%, 1%) level (two-tailed). All continuous variables are trimmed at the 0.5%. The t-statistics in parentheses are calculated using robust standard errors clustered by the firm. In this table, every given firm is represented as many times as CDS spreads are available for that company. The coefficients of year, and industry are suppressed. The independent variables are STICKY and control variables as defined in Table 4.2.

Quarter Effects

Since my sample is based on quarterly data, in addition to firm and year fixed effects or firm random, year and industry fixed effects I include quarter fixed effects to control for seasonal effects, as they may influence the results. Table 4.9 provides evidence that the results remain qualitatively similar to the main results in Table 4.3.

Table 4.9: Robustness based on quarter & firm fixed effects and quarter & industry fixed effects for the sample covering 5-year CDS contracts

		LOG_CDS			
Variable	Exp. sign	(1)	(2)	(3)	(4)
STICKY	+	0.0433**	0.0709***	0.0428**	0.0683***
		(2.22)	(4.66)	(2.22)	(4.59)
LEV	+		0.8526*		1.2286***
			(1.92)		(3.73)
RF	-		-0.1449***		-0.1384***
			(-4.02)		(-3.72)
VOL	+		15.4518***		16.9469***
			(7.00)		(8.38)
SENIORITY	-		-0.2413***		-0.2322***
			(-7.37)		(-7.14)

Table 4.9 continued

CUMR	+		0.0520***		0.0555***
			(4.43)		(4.58)
EXR	-		-0.0488***		-0.0414***
			(-3.11)		(-2.59)
SIZE	-		-0.4777***		-0.3891***
			(-5.72)		(-6.91)
ROA	-		0.5298		-0.8065
			(0.23)		(-0.36)
Constant	+/-	4.6785***	4.8748***	5.0167***	5.1378***
		(28.58)	(27.70)	(18.54)	(14.08)
N		2,906	2,906	2,906	2,906
Number of firms		130	130	130	130
Firm FE		YES	YES	NO	NO
Year FE		YES	YES	YES	YES
Quarter FE		YES	YES	YES	YES
Industry FE		NO	NO	YES	YES
Adjusted R^2		0.1230	0.6463	0.4558	0.6998

Table 4.9 presents results of the effect of cost stickiness on 5–year CDS spreads using quarter & firm fixed effects and quarter & industry fixed effects. The dependent variable is log of CDS premium one working day after the SEC filing. Column 1 shows the results for the regression of credit spreads on cost stickiness, firm, year, and quarter fixed effects without controls. Column 2 shows the results for the model, which augments the Column 1 with controls. Column 3 shows the results for the regression of credit spreads on cost stickiness, year, quarter, industry fixed and firm random effects without controls. Column 4 shows the results for the model, which augments the Column 3 with controls. *(**, ***) Denotes significance at the 10% (5%, 1%) level (two-tailed). All continuous variables are trimmed at the 0.5%. The t-statistics in parentheses are calculated using robust standard errors clustered by the firm. In this table, every given firm is represented as many times as CDS spreads are available for that company. The coefficients of firm, year, quarter, and industry are suppressed. The independent variables are STICKY and control variables as defined in Table 4.2.

Seniority

In the following, I divide the main 5-year maturity CDS sample into two subsamples based on the seniority of the debt and confirm the positive relation between cost stickiness and credit risk within each subsample. Panel A of Table 4.10 presents results for senior debt and Panel B for subordinated debt. The effect of cost stickiness is as expected positive and statistically significant at the 1% level in the subsample with senior as well as with subordinated debt. The coefficients of the control variables and their significance are comparable to the main results.

Table 4.10: Robustness based on seniority/subordination for the sample covering 5-year CDS contracts

Panel A: Sample covers senior debt only

		LOG_CDS	
Variable	Exp. sign	(1)	(2)
STICKY	+	0.0670***	0.0656***
		(4.30)	(4.32)
LEV	+	0.9908**	1.3163***
		(2.19)	(4.01)
RF	-	-0.1439***	-0.1331***
		(-4.01)	(-3.62)
VOL	+	15.4254***	17.0219***
		(6.73)	(8.26)
CUMR	+	0.0558***	0.0592***
		(4.88)	(5.00)
EXR	-	-0.0481***	-0.0401***
		(-3.33)	(-2.70)
SIZE	-	-0.5246***	-0.4562***
		(-6.69)	(-9.44)
ROA	-	0.2965	-0.7751
		(0.13)	(-0.35)
Constant	+/-	4.5858***	4.6196***
		(28.99)	(29.45)

Table 4.10 continued

	(1)	(2)
N	2,303	2,303
Number of firms	128	128
Firm FE	YES	NO
Year FE	YES	YES
Quarter FE	YES	YES
Adjusted R^2	0.5715	0.5699

Panel B: Sample covers subordinated debt only

Variable	Exp. sign	(1)	(2)
STICKY	+	0.0737***	0.0743***
		(2.95)	(2.94)
LEV	+	-0.1559	1.2198**
		(-0.19)	(2.31)
RF	-	-0.1738***	-0.1649***
		(-2.81)	(-2.81)
VOL	+	11.2132***	12.2190***
		(3.64)	(4.37)
CUMR	+	0.0885***	0.1029***
		(3.50)	(3.88)
EXR	-	-0.0022	0.0318
		(-0.06)	(0.83)
SIZE	-	-0.3186*	-0.2904***
		(-1.99)	(-4.36)
ROA	-	-0.8091	0.3296
		(-0.36)	(0.17)
Constant	+/-	5.1985***	5.1763***
		(17.05)	(18.44)
N		603	603

Table 4.10 continued

Number of firms	65	65
Firm FE	YES	NO
Year FE	YES	YES
Quarter FE	YES	YES
Adjusted R^2	0.6188	0.6084

Table 4.10 presents the robustness based on the seniority/subordination. Panel A shows the results for the sample covering 5-year CDS contracts on senior debt. In Column 1 the CDS spreads are regressed on cost stickiness, firm, year, and quarter fixed effects, and controls. In Column 2 the CDS spreads are regressed on cost stickiness, firm random, year and quarter fixed effects, and controls.

Panel B shows the results for the sample covering 5-year CDS contracts on subordinated debt. In Column 1 the CDS spreads are regressed on cost stickiness, firm, year, and quarter fixed effects, and controls. In Column 2 the CDS spreads are regressed on cost stickiness, firm random, year and quarter fixed effects, and controls. *(**, ***) Denotes significance at the 10% (5%, 1%) level (two-tailed). All continuous variables are trimmed at the 0.5%. The t-statistics in parentheses are calculated using robust standard errors clustered by the firm. In this table, every given firm is represented as many times as CDS spreads are available for that company. The coefficients of firm, year, and quarter are suppressed. The dependent variable is log of CDS premium one working day after the SEC filing. The independent variables are STICKY and control variables as defined in Table 4.2

Sticky Dummy

In Table 4.11 I replace the continuous STICKY variable with a dummy variable (D_STICKY) equal to one if a firm is exhibiting sticky cost behavior (STICKY > 0) and zero otherwise. The main effect becomes even stronger; the coefficient of D_STICKY varies from 0.1116 to 0.1418 depending on the model specification and is highly significant at the 1% level confirming my main finding in Table 4.3. Further, to allow a more direct interpretation of the effect of cost stickiness on credit risk, I measure the dependent variable in basis points (i.e., without taking the logarithm). This analysis based on the model presented in Column 2, shows that firms with sticky costs exhibit on average 38 basis points higher CDS spreads.[160]

[160] The results are shown in Appendix 5, Table A.2.

Table 4.11: Robustness based on a dummy variable for cost stickiness for the sample covering 5-year CDS contracts

Variable	Exp. sign	LOG_CDS (1)	(2)	(3)	(4)	(5)
D_STICKY	+	0.1138***	0.1418***	0.1162***	0.1116***	0.1316***
		(3.21)	(4.71)	(3.29)	(3.17)	(4.47)
LEV	+		0.9291**			1.2853***
			(2.09)			(3.81)
RF	-		-0.1463***			-0.1393***
			(-4.02)			(-3.72)
VOL	+		15.3315***			16.8056***
			(6.88)			(8.15)
SENIORITY	-		-0.2425***			-0.2336***
			(-7.48)			(-7.24)
CUMR	+		0.0531***			0.0568***
			(4.44)			(4.61)
EXR	-		-0.0492***			-0.0417**
			(-3.01)			(-2.52)
SIZE	-		-0.4659***			-0.3822***
			(-5.42)			(-6.49)
ROA	-		1.7002			0.3717
			(0.75)			(0.17)
Constant	+/-	4.6148***	4.8037***	4.7751***	4.9524***	5.0547***
		(28.65)	(26.75)	(27.62)	(18.54)	(14.04)
N		2,906	2,906	2,906	2,906	2,906
Number of firms		130	130	130	130	130
Firm FE		YES	YES	NO	NO	NO
Year FE		YES	YES	YES	YES	YES
Quarter FE		YES	YES	YES	YES	YES
Industry FE		NO	NO	NO	YES	YES

Table 4.11 continued

Adjusted R^2	0.1240	0.6465	0.1244	0.4549	0.6974

Table 4.11 presents the results of the effect of sticky dummy on 5–year CDS spreads using year, quarter & firm fixed effects and year, quarter & industry fixed effects. The dependent variable is log of CDS premium one working day after the SEC filing. Column 1 shows the results for the regression of credit spreads on sticky dummy, firm, year, and quarter fixed effects without controls. Column 2 shows the results for the model, which augments the Column 1 with controls. Column 3 shows the results for the regression of credit spreads on sticky dummy, year, and quarter fixed and firm random effects without controls. Column 4 shows the results for the regression of credit spreads on sticky dummy, year, quarter, and industry fixed effects without controls. Column 5 shows the results for the model, which augments the Column 4 with controls. *(**, ***) Denotes significance at the 10% (5%, 1%) level (two-tailed). All continuous variables are trimmed at the 0.5%. The t-statistics in parentheses are calculated using robust standard errors clustered by the firm. In this table, every given firm is represented as many times as CDS spreads are available for that company. The coefficients of firm, year, quarter, and industry are suppressed. The independent variables are STICKY and control variables as defined in Table 4.2.

Outlier Treatment

To test the sensitivity of the results to different outlier treatments, I winsorize at the 0.5% level. Table 4.12 shows the results, which do not change qualitatively compared to the main results.

Table 4.12: Robustness based on alternative outlier treatment for the sample covering 5-year CDS contracts

		LOG_CDS	
Variable	Exp. sign	(1)	(2)
STICKY	+	0.0307*	0.0537***
		(1.79)	(3.87)
LEV	+		0.7223*
			(1.74)
RF	-		-0.1214***
			(-3.20)
VOL	+		13.1445***
			(7.36)

Table 4.12 continued

SENIORITY	-		-0.2409***
			(-7.74)
CUMR	+		0.0484***
			(4.02)
EXR	-		-0.0435***
			(-2.71)
SIZE	-		-0.4940***
			(-6.64)
ROA	-		0.4084
			(0.27)
Constant	+/-	4.7433***	4.8627***
		(30.34)	(30.15)
N		3,102	3,102
Number of firms		133	133
Firm FE		YES	YES
Year FE		YES	YES
Adjusted R^2		0.3580	0.5828

Table 4.12 presents results of the effect of cost stickiness on 5–year CDS spreads. The dependent variable is log of CDS premium one working day after the SEC filing. Column 1 shows the results for the regression of credit spreads on cost stickiness, firm random and year fixed effects without controls. Column 2 shows the results for the model, which augments the Column 1 with controls. *(**, ***) Denotes significance at the 10% (5%, 1%) level (two-tailed). All continuous variables are winsorized at the 0.5%. The t-statistics in parentheses are calculated using robust standard errors clustered by the firm. In this table, every given firm is represented as many times as CDS spreads are available for that company. The coefficients of year and firm are suppressed. The independent variables are STICKY and control variables as defined in Table 4.2.

Further, I repeat the analysis without removing the outliers, trim and alternatively winsorize at the 1% level. My results do not change qualitatively compared to the outlier treatment in the main specification, where I trim at the 0.5% level.

Overall, the robustness checks support the main finding of a positive relation of asymmetric cost behavior on credit risk and provide evidence that my results are not driven by the implemented methodology.

4.7 Summary and Conclusion

This chapter examines the direct relation between cost stickiness and credit risk. Based on prior research I argue that cost stickiness will lead to higher earnings volatility, higher accounting information risk, and under some conditions to higher future earnings. While the first and second channel will increase a firm's default probability and thus credit risk, the third channel will reduce credit risk. I expect that the first two channels will dominate the third and therefore stickiness should increase credit risk. To test this hypothesis, I use 2,906 5-year and 23,765 6-months to 30-years CDS contracts from 2001 to 2011. The results suggest that the increase in asset volatility and higher accounting information risk dominate the potential increase in asset value as expected and hence credit risk increases with cost stickiness after controlling for well-known CDS determinants and various model specifications. Further, I document that the effect of cost stickiness is stronger for short-term maturities, being consistent with the observation that cost stickiness has a short-term impact. My results are also robust to a specification, in which I lag the main independent variable (STICKY) to reduce reverse causality concerns.

With this finding, I contribute to the accounting and finance literature. Regarding the accounting literature, I extend the cost asymmetry literature by providing a credit risk implication of sticky cost behavior. In particular, I document that sticky firms are more likely to cross the default boundary because of weaker cost control, higher earnings volatility, and poorer earnings quality. Regarding the finance literature, I contribute to the credit derivatives literature by showing that costs matter in CDS pricing.

My finding of a negative credit market response to cost stickiness also is of practical relevance for managers. One practical implication is that when managers keep excess resources in declining sales periods their firms' credit risk increases and therefore their firms' financing costs rise as well. Another practical implication is that my findings can help creditors, analysts, and credit rating agencies to predict credit risk related to asymmetric cost decisions.

5 Does Cost Stickiness Affect Financial Risk?

In this chapter I investigate the impact of asymmetric cost behavior on financial risk. Figure 5.1 illustrates the structure of this chapter.

Figure 5.1: Structure of Chapter 5

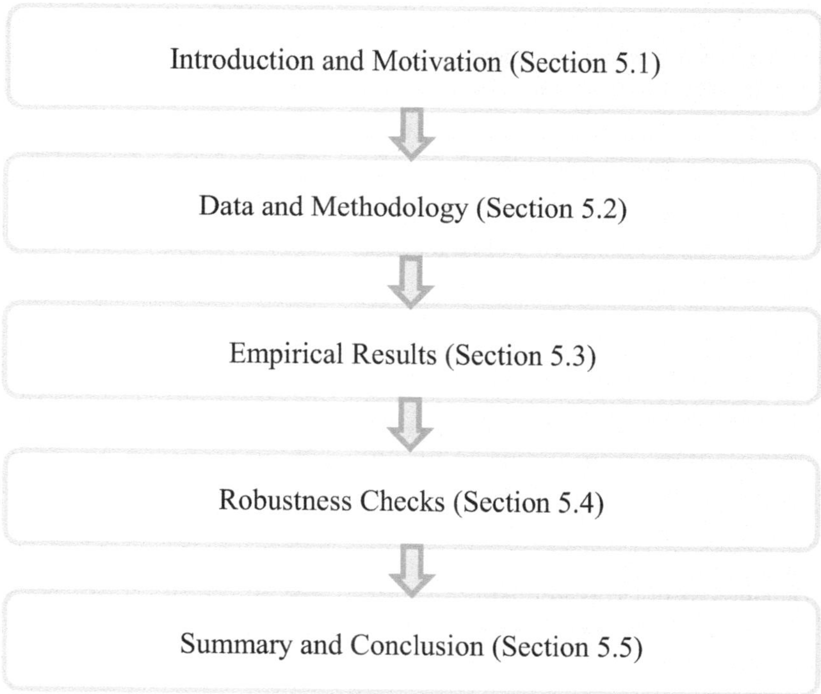

5.1 Introduction and Motivation

As discussed in Chapter 4, asymmetric cost behavior can be interpreted as an investment in a risky project. Thus, cost stickiness can be thought as part of a firm's overall business risk defined as "the risk associated with the level and stability of

K. Reimer, *Asymmetric Cost Behavior*, Quantitatives Controlling,
https://doi.org/10.1007/978-3-658-22822-4_5

operating cash flow".[161] The business risk of a firm is exposed to market risk, i.e., a potential loss from unfavorable market movements, usually estimated as risk from a stock market index such as the S&P 500 in the US market or EURO STOXX 50 in the European market.[162] The finance theory postulates that a firm's business risk is shared between equity and debt holders.[163] When a firm is a pure equity firm, the equity holders alone assume the business risk. When a firm is partially financed by debt and the risk of default is present, the debt holders assume part of the business risk and have to be compensated by a fixed payment. The equity holders have claims on the residual value of a firm's assets. Thus, the equity and debt holders share the value of a firm as well as its overall business risk.[164] Crouhy, Galai, and Mark (2001) define this "sharing rule" as "financial risk",[165] which is affected by the capital structure and the financial leverage of a firm. Figure 5.2 visualizes the relationships between market risk, business risk, default, and financial risk of a firm.

Figure 5.2: Relationships between Market Risk, Business Risk, Default Risk, and Financial Risk

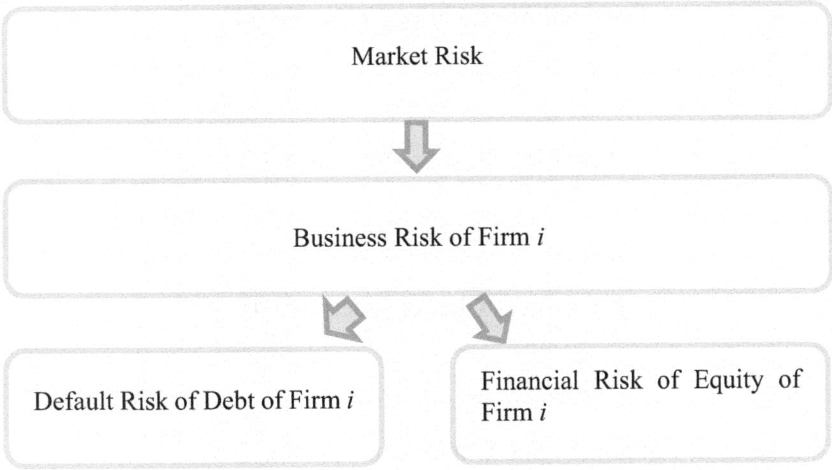

Source: based on Crouhy, Galai, and Mark (2001), p. 683.

161 Crouphy, Galai, and Mark (2001), p. 313.
162 The market risk can be thought as conglomerate of interest rate risk, equity price risk, foreign exchange risk, and commodity risk. For details see e.g., Crouphy, Galai, and Mark (2001), pp. 177-179.
163 See e.g. Crouphy, Galai, and Mark (2001), p. 683.
164 See Crouphy, Galai, and Mark (2001), p. 686.
165 See Crouphy, Galai, and Mark (2001), p. 687.

The riskiness of future cash flows resulting from sticky cost behavior should result in higher compensation for the stockholders. In Chapter 4 I documented that cost stickiness increases credit spreads, and thus the default risk of a firm. In the following I test empirically whether cost stickiness influences the expected cost of equity and thus the financial risk of a firm.

5.2 Data and Methodology

5.2.1 Sample Selection

I utilize the data for the years 1974 through 2015 from a combination of four data sources: Standard and Poor's Compustat, the Center for Research in Security Prices, the Federal Reserve Bank Reports, and Kenneth French's library.

To estimate the equity cost of capital I obtain monthly returns for US firms with ordinary shares (CRSP share codes 10 or 11) from the CRSP monthly stock file which are subsequently merged with the Fama French factors. To avoid distortions caused by outliers I delete the observations with returns in the extreme top and bottom one percentile.

I calculate the main variable of interests, cost stickiness, on the quarterly basis using the Standard and Poors's Compustat - Fundamentals Annual data source. To estimate the standard deviation of returns I obtain the daily returns from the CRSP daily stock file for US firms with ordinary shares (CRSP share codes 10 or 11) from January 1974 to 2015. Finally, the compounding yearly equity costs of capital, the annualized standard deviation of equity returns and the cost stickiness measure at the end of the fiscal year are merged with the annual Compustat database. The final sample consists of firm-year observations whereby I implement the following restrictions:

I exclude companies in the financial industry and utilities industry, i.e. with Standard Industrial Classification (SIC) codes from 6000 through 6999 and from 4900 through 4999 respectively.

I restrict the sample to the observations with positive book value.

I exclude observations with a share price of less than $1.

I winsorize the values of cost of equity to be between 0 and 1.

I exclude observations with missing values of one of the variables required in the regression 5.4.

The final sample contains 27,099 observations representing 4,735 unique firms. Depending on the analysis, in most regressions the sample ranges from 1979 to 2012, due to the need of the data for 60 preceding and 36 following months.

5.2.2 Methodology

In order to show how cost stickiness affects the financial risk of equity I analyze the relationship between cost stickiness and the expected cost of equity.

The cost of equity measure is calculated using Fama French Three Factor Model (Fama and French 1993). To estimate the factor loadings for each firm *i*, I regress the monthly time series of stock returns on the Fama French factors market (*RMRF*), firm size (*SMB*), and value (*HML*) using monthly data from year $t + 1$ to year $t + 3$:[166]

$$return_{i,m} - r_m^f = \alpha_i + \beta_i^{Market} \cdot RMRF_m + \beta_i^{Size} \cdot SMB_m + \beta_i^{Value} \cdot HML_m + \varepsilon_{i,m} \quad 5.1$$

with:

$return_{i,m}$ = return of firm *i* during month *m*

r_m^f = riskless rate during month *m*

$RMRF_m$ = excess return of the market portfolio over riskless rate during month *m*

SMB_m = return difference between small and large capitalization stocks during month m

HML_m = return difference between high and low book-to-market stocks during month *m*

β_i^l = loading of firm *i* on factor l.

Using the estimated factor loadings from regression 5.1, I then calculate the expected cost of equity in year *t* as follows:

166 The data as well the details of exact calculation of the factor mimicking portfolios are available in Kenneth R. French's data library at http://mba.tuck.dartmouth.edu/pages/faculty/ken.french/data_library.html.

$$COE_{i,t} = \overline{r_t^f} + \hat{\beta}_{i,t}^{Market} \cdot \overline{RMRF_t} + \hat{\beta}_{i,t}^{Size} \cdot \overline{SMB_t} + \hat{\beta}_{i,t}^{Value} \cdot \overline{HML_t}, \qquad 5.2$$

where $\overline{r_t^f}$, $\overline{RMRF_t}$, $\overline{SMB_t}$, and $\overline{HML_t}$ are expected annual factor returns for year $t+1$. To estimate the expected annual factor returns, I apply the approach of Barth, Konchitchki, and Landsman (2013). First, I calculate the average monthly returns over the 60 months prior to month m for $\overline{RMRF_t}$, $\overline{SMB_t}$, and $\overline{HML_t}$ and over the 12 months for $\overline{r_t^f}$.[167] Next, I compound the average monthly returns over the twelve months prior to the beginning of firm i's fiscal year.

To evaluate the impact of cost stickiness on expected cost of capital I conduct two types of regressions. First, I apply the Fama-MacBeth approach following Fama and MacBeth (1973). In this approach, I run t cross-sectional regressions, i.e., for each point of time. Then I compute the average of the t estimated coefficients. Since the standard errors are calculated using the time-series of the estimated coefficients, the standard errors account for the "time effect", i.e., correlation across different firms at a given point of time.[168] Petersen (2009) advocates the use of regressions with standard errors that are clustered by firm in addition to time, i.e., account for correlation across time for a given firm, calling it a "firm effect". Therefore, in addition to the Fama-MacBeth regression I run OLS regressions with standard errors clustered by firm and time.

Eq. 5.3 measures the impact of cost stickiness on expected cost of equity, where cost stickiness (STICKY) is calculated in the same manner as in Chapter 4 following Weiss (2010). Eq. 5.4 extends Eq. 5.3 by adding the fundamental characteristics: the CAPM beta (BETA) the natural logarithm of market value (LOGSIZE), and the equity book-to-market ratio (BM):

$$COE_{i,t+1} = \alpha_0 + \alpha_1 STICKY_{i,t} + \varepsilon_{i,t+1}. \qquad 5.3$$

$$COE_{i,t+1} = \alpha_0 + \alpha_1 STICKY_{i,t} + \alpha_2 BETA_{i,t} + \alpha_3 LOGSIZE_{i,t} + \alpha_4 BM_{i,t} + \varepsilon_{i,t+1}. \qquad 5.4$$

The empirical evidence that cost stickiness captures dimensions of risk incremental to the Fama French factors is given by a positive value of α_1 in Eq. 5.4.

---

167 The risk-free rate is calculated based on the shorter time period to rule out the outdated estimates.

168 See Petersen (2009), p. 436 for the definition of time effect.

5.3 Empirical Results

5.3.1 Descriptive Statistics

Table 5.1 summarizes the descriptive statistics of the variables used in the regression analysis. The mean (median) cost of equity amounts to 14.80 (12.00)%.[169] The mean market value of analyzed firms amounts to 2,477 (168) million US$ and is comparable with other descriptive statistics reported (e.g., Bonenkamp, Homburg, and Kempf 2009).[170] 51.1% of firms exhibit sticky costs with the average mean within the whole sample equal to 0.016.

Table 5.1: Descriptive statistics of the main variables

Variable	N	Mean	SD	Q1	Median	Q3
MV	27,099	2,477.319	13,486.720	43.381	168.069	856.452
LOGSIZE	27,099	5.389	2.000	3.769	5.124	6.753
COE	27,099	0.148	0.137	0.039	0.120	0.220
STICKY	27,099	0.016	1.095	-0.390	0.011	0.440
D_STICKY	27,099	0.511	0.500	0.000	0.000	1.000
BM	27,099	0.753	0.598	0.360	0.608	0.962
BETA	27,099	1.042	0.558	0.667	1.013	1.375

MV	Market value (in $MM) of equity calculated as close price multiplied by common shares outstanding at the end of the fiscal year;
LOGSIZE	Log of market value of equity at the fiscal year end;
COE	Expected annual cost of equity;
STICKY	Sticky measure on an annual basis. It is calculated as: $STICKY_{i,t} = -[\log(\Delta COST/\Delta SALE)_{i,\underline{\tau}} - \log(\Delta COST/\Delta SALE)_{i,\overline{\tau}}]$, with $\underline{\tau}, \overline{\tau} \in \{t,..,t-3\}$; $\underline{\tau}$ is the most recent of the last four years with a decrease in sales and $\overline{\tau}$ is most recent of the last four years with an

169 When I summarize the cost of equity by industry, I observe the lowest cost of equity in "Candy and Soda" (9.67%) and "Personal Services" (11.75%) and the highest in "Construction" (19.23%) and "Precious Metals" (22.49%).

170 It should be noted that the average market value of firms reported in Chapter 4 is considerably larger. This consideration can be attributed to the fact that CDSs are mostly bought for significantly large firms.

	increase in sales. COST = sales – earnings;
D_STICKY	An indicator variable equal to 1 if STICKY > 0 and 0 otherwise;
BM	Book-to-market ratio calculated as common equity divided by market value at the fiscal year end;
BETA	CAPM beta

5.3.2 Regression Results

Table 5.2 presents the results of Eqs. 5.3 and 5.4. As predicted, the asymmetric cost behavior is positively related to the cost of equity at the 1% level. When I control for Fama French fundamental risk characteristics, the coefficient of STICKY decreases from 0.0046 to 0.0026, remaining highly statistically significant at the 1% level. These results demonstrate that cost stickiness comprises some dimension of risk, which is not captured by Fama French factors. Further, the lower statistical significance of STICKY when the fundamental characteristics are included indicates that cost stickiness and Fama French characteristics are correlated and reflect some common information about cost of equity. Overall, the results show that cost stickiness reflects information with regard to the cost of equity incremental to that captured by Fama French characteristics.

Table 5.2: Cost stickiness and the expected cost of equity

Panel A: OLS regressions with adjusted standard errors

Variable	Exp. sign	COE (1)	COE (2)
STICKY	+	0.0041***	0.0026***
		(5.30)	(3.45)
BETA	+		0.0209***
			(13.52)
LOGSIZE	-		-0.0107***
			(-24.07)
BM	+		0.0174***
			(10.34)

Table 5.2 continued

Constant	+/-	0.1484***	0.1712***
		(178.32)	(49.52)
N		27,099	27,099
Adjusted R^2		0.0010	0.0428

Panel B: Fama-MacBeth regressions

Variable	Exp. sign	COE (1)	COE (2)
STICKY	+	0.0030**	0.0022*
		(2.25)	(1.91)
BETA	+		0.0208***
			(4.08)
LOGSIZE	-		-0.0032
			(--1.14)
BM	+		0.0099***
			(4.37)
Constant	+/-	0.1605***	0.1412***
		(11.53)	(7.63)
N		27,099	27,099
Adjusted R^2		0.0039	0.0760

Table 5.2 presents results of the effect of cost stickiness on the expected cost of equity. Panel A reports the results for OLS regressions with standard errors clustered by firm and year. Panel B reports the results for Fama-MacBeth regressions. COE is the expected cost of capital based on Fama French Three Factor Model. STICKY is the cost stickiness measure following Weiss (2010). BETA is the CAPM beta. LOGSIZE is the logarithm of equity market value. BM is the book-to-market value of equity. *(**, ***) Denotes significance at the 10% (5%, 1%) level (two-tailed). All continuous variables are winsorized at the 1% level but COE between 0 and 1. The t-statistics in parentheses are calculated using robust standard errors clustered by firm and year in OLS regression or is the Fama-MacBeth (1973) t-statistics.

To enable the comparability of each explanators' importance, I standardize all independent variables and estimate the regressions once more.[171] The results are shown in Table 5.3 below. The standardized effect of cost stickiness on expected cost of equity is almost identical in OLS and Fama-MacBeth specifications. One standard deviation increase in cost stickiness leads to an increase of expected cost of equity by 0.0218 (0.0183) standard deviations in an OLS (Fama-MacBeth) specification. The largest standardized effect on expected cost of equity is attributed to the size of a firm in OLS regression and to CAPM beta in Fama-MacBeth regression. Overall the results show that cost stickiness has both a statistically and relatively modest practical significant impact on the expected cost of equity.

Table 5.3: Standardized impact of cost stickiness on the expected cost of equity

		COE	
Variable	Exp. sign	OLS	Fama-MacBeth
STICKY	+	0.0218***	0.0183*
		(3.45)	(1.91)
BETA	+	0.0897***	0.0892***
		(13.52)	(4.08)
LOGSIZE	-	-0.1616***	-0.0485
		(-24.07)	(-1.14)
BM	+	0.0777***	0.0443***
		(10.34)	(4.37)
Constant	+/-	0.0165***	0.0665
		(2.77)	(0.79)
N		27,099	27,099
Adjusted R^2		0.0428	0.0760

171 In a standard OLS the magnitudes of coefficients can be changed by altering the units of measurement of a determinant. Thus, it is not possible to interpret the relative importance of an independent variable based on the value of estimated coefficient, rather when each variable has been standardized (see, Wooldridge 2013, p. 182).

Table 5.3 presents results of the effect of cost stickiness on expected cost of equity, where all variables are standardized by subtracting their means and dividing these by their standard deviation. COE is the standardized expected cost of capital based on the Fama French Three Factor Model. STICKY is the cost stickiness measure following Weiss (2010). BETA is the standardized CAPM beta. LOGSIZE is the standardized logarithm of equity market value. BM is the standardized book-to-market value of equity. *(**, ***) Denotes significance at the 10% (5%, 1%) level (two-tailed). All continuous variables are winsorized at the 1% but COE between 0 and 1. The t-statistics in parentheses are calculated using robust standard errors clustered by the firm and year in OLS regression or is the Fama-MacBeth (1973) t-statistics.

5.3.3 Extended model

As previously explained, in the presence of risk of default, the equity and debtholders share the business risk while the equity holders are exposed to financial risk and the debt holders to the risk of default. The extent of financial risk, i.e., the uncertainty regarding the claims on the firm's assets, depends on the capital structure of the firm and its financial leverage. Fama and French (1996) proposed that size and book-to-market factors capture the financial risk. Vassalou and Xing (2004) document that although these factors contain default-related information as well as other significant price information, the default factor in addition to the Fama French factors helps to predict the equity returns more precisely. Thus, to rule out that cost stickiness subsumes financial risk captured by leverage, I control for leverage, measured as total debt divided by the market value of assets (computed as market value of equity plus total liabilities) at fiscal year-end.

Recent empirical research shows that profitability is positively related to future equity returns (e.g., Fama and French 2006, 2008; Chen, Novy-Marx, and Zhang 2011; Novy-Marx 2013). The explanation for the profitability premium is based on the dividend discount model, in which the market value of a firm's stock is the present value of expected dividends. With clean surplus accounting, the dividends can be replaced by equity earnings per share less the change in book equity per share. Dividing by book equity allows for predictions regarding the expected earnings and expected stock returns: firms with higher expected earnings relative to current book equity earn higher expected returns controlling for book-to-market and expected growth in book equity.[172]

172 See Fama and French (2015), p. 492.

In contrast to equity markets, credit markets face a negative profitability premium. Since debt holders are concerned with downside risk and that profitability decreases the probability to default and increases firms' liquidity, the profitability is negatively related to credit spreads (e.g., Callen, Livnat, and Segal 2009; Campbell, Chichernea, and Petkevitch 2016). In turn equity holders are the residual claimants, thus they are concerned with both the upside potential of highly profitable firms and the downside, i.e., distress risk of less profitable firms.[173] In a recent study, Campbell, Chichernea, and Petkevitch (2016) document that profitability comprises partially offsetting information about the default risk (decreasing equity returns) and the riskiness of the firm's future cash flow (increasing equity returns). The authors conclude that the overall impact of profitability on equity returns depends on the relative importance of default risk and the riskiness of the firm's future cash flow. Thus, without predicting the direction of profitability and equity returns association, I control for profitability measured as income before extraordinary items scaled by previous book value of total assets.

Next, as discussed in Chapter 4, cost stickiness may affect volatility, information asymmetry, as well as current and expected earnings, which in turn determine the default and financial risks. To ensure the accuracy of prediction of the multiple regression model, I residualize the correlated predictor variables by running the following regressions $Control_{i,t} = \alpha_0 + \alpha_1 STICKY_{i,t} +$ year fixed effects $+\varepsilon_{i,t}$ and use the error terms as proxies for each control variable, where $Control_{i,t}$ is firm beta, logarithm of market value, book-to-market ratio, leverage, or return on assets.

The extended model is presented by Eq. 5.5.

$$\begin{aligned} COE_{i,t+1} = {} & \alpha_0 + \alpha_1 STICKY_{i,t} + \alpha_2 BETA\_R_{i,t} \\ & + \alpha_3 LOGSIZE\_R_{i,t} + \alpha_4 BM\_R_{i,t} \\ & + \alpha_5 LEV\_R_{i,t} + \alpha_6 ROA\_R_{i,t} + \varepsilon_{i,t+1}. \end{aligned} \quad (5.5)$$

The results of Eq. 5.5 are presented in Table 5.4 below. As predicted, cost stickiness increases the expected cost of equity after controlling for various determinants of equity costs. The coefficient of STICKY is highly significant in the OLS regression at the 1% level and at the 5% level in the Fama-MacBeth results. The differences in the level and significance of coefficients in the OLS and Fama-MacBeth regressions are attributed to different estimation procedures. While the OLS method estimates a sample specific coefficient, the Fama-MacBeth approach estimates year specific coefficients averaged to one sample specific coefficient.

173 See Campbell, Chichernea, and Petkevitch (2016), p. 103.

Table 5.4: Impact of cost stickiness on the expected cost of equity controlling for leverage and profitability

		COE	
Variable	Exp. sign	OLS	Fama-MacBeth
STICKY	+	0.0043***	0.0038**
		(4.65)	(2.34)
BETA_R	+	0.0123***	0.0203***
		(6.32)	(3.95)
LOGSIZE_R	-	-0.0006	-0.0025
		(-1.13)	(-0.91)
BM_R	+	0.0026	0.0021
		(1.18)	(0.80)
LEV_R	+	0.0590***	0.0542***
		(7.12)	(4.92)
ROA_R	+/-	-0.0646***	-0.0766***
		(-4.94)	(-2.85)
Constant	+/-	0.1433***	0.1548***
		(148.46)	(11.66)
N		18,188	18,188
Adjusted R^2		0.0110	0.0975

Table 5.4 presents results of the effect of cost stickiness on the expected cost of equity using the extended model (Eq. 5.5). *COE* is the expected cost of capital based on the Fama French Three Factor Model. STICKY is the cost stickiness measure following Weiss (2010). BETA_R is the residual from the following regression: $Beta_{i,t} = \alpha_0 + \alpha_1 STICKY_{i,t} + \text{year fixed effects} + \varepsilon_{i,t}$ where BETA is CAPM beta. LOGSIZE_R is the residual from the following cross-sectional regression:
$LOGSIZE_{i,t} = \alpha_0 + \alpha_1 STICKY_{i,t} + \text{year fixed effects} + \varepsilon_{i,t}$ where LOGSIZE is the logarithm of equity market value. BM_R is the residual from
$BM_{i,t} = \alpha_0 + \alpha_1 STICKY_{i,t} + \text{year fixed effects} + \varepsilon_{i,t}$ where BM is the book-to-market value of equity.

Table 5.4 continued

LEV_R is the residual from the following cross-sectional regression: $LEV_{i,t} = \alpha_0 + \alpha_1 STICKY_{i,t} + \text{year fixed effects} + \varepsilon_{i,t}$ where LEV is the leverage measured as total debt divided by market value of assets. ROA_R is the residual from the following cross-sectional regression: $ROA_{i,t} = \alpha_0 + \alpha_1 STICKY_{i,t} + \text{year fixed effects} + \varepsilon_{i,t}$ where ROA is the return on assets, measured as income before extraordinary items scaled by the previous book value of total assets.

*(**, ***) Denotes significance at the 10% (5%, 1%) level (two-tailed). All continuous variables are winsorized at the 1% but COE between 0 and 1. The t-statistics in parentheses are calculated using robust standard errors clustered by the firm and year in OLS regression or is the Fama-MacBeth (1973) t-statistics.

Table 5.5 below summarizes the results for the standardized impact of asymmetric cost behavior on the expected cost of equity in the extended model. The relative impact of sticky costs is almost identical in the OLS and Fama-MacBeth specifications. One standard deviation increase in cost stickiness leads to 0.0357 (0.0315) standard deviations increase in the expected cost of equity in the OLS (Fama-MacBeth) specification. The largest standardized effect on the expected cost of equity is attributed to the leverage of a firm in OLS regression and to CAPM beta in Fama-MacBeth regression.

Table 5.5: Standardized impact of cost stickiness on the expected cost of equity in the extended model

Variable	Exp. sign	ECC OLS	ECC Fama-MacBeth
STICKY_R	+	0.0357***	0.0315**
		(4.65)	(2.34)
BETA_R	+	0.0508***	0.0840***
		(6.32)	(3.95)
LOGSIZE_R	-	-0.0090	-0.0355
		(-1.13)	(-0.91)
BM_R	+	0.0113	0.0089
		(1.18)	(0.80)
LEV_R	+	0.0617***	0.0567***
		(7.12)	(4.92)
ROA_R	+/-	-0.0386***	-0.0458***
		(-4.94)	(-2.85)
Constant	+/-	0.0007	0.0873
		(0.09)	(0.87)
N		18,188	18,188
Adjusted R^2		0.0110	0.0975

Table 5.5 presents results of the effect of cost stickiness on the expected cost of equity, where all variables are standardized by subtracting their means and dividing these by their standard deviation. COE is the standardized expected cost of capital based on the Fama French Three Factor Model. STICKY is the cost stickiness measure following Weiss (2010). BETA_R is the standardized residual from the following regression: $Beta_{i,t} = \alpha_0 + \alpha_1 STICKY_{i,t} +$ year fixed effects $+\varepsilon_{i,t}$ where BETA is the CAPM beta. LOGSIZE_R is the standardized residual from the following cross-sectional regression:
$LOGSIZE_{i,t} = \alpha_0 + \alpha_1 STICKY_{i,t} +$ year fixed effects $+ \varepsilon_{i,t}$ where LOGSIZE is the logarithm of equity market value. BM_R is the standardized residual from $BM_{i,t} = \alpha_0 + \alpha_1 STICKY_{i,t} +$ year fixed effects $+ \varepsilon_{i,t}$ where BM is the book-to-market value of equity.

Table 5.5 continued

LEV_R is the standardized residual from the following cross-sectional regression: $LEV_{i,t} = \alpha_0 + \alpha_1 STICKY_{i,t} + \text{year fixed effects} + \varepsilon_{i,t}$ where LEV is the leverage measured as total debt divided by market value of assets. ROA_R is the standardized residual from the following cross-sectional regression: $ROA_{i,t} = \alpha_0 + \alpha_1 STICKY_{i,t} + \text{year fixed effects} + \varepsilon_{i,t}$ where ROA is the return on assets, measured as income before extraordinary items scaled by the previous book value of total assets. *(**, ***) Denotes significance at the 10% (5%, 1%) level (two-tailed). All continuous variables are winsorized at the 1% but COE between 0 and 1. The t-statistics in parentheses are calculated using robust standard errors clustered by the firm and year in OLS regression or is the Fama-MacBeth (1973) t-statistics.

5.3.4 Addressing Endogeneity Concerns

To mitigate the concern of reverse causality, which would bias the results, I lag main independent variable and re-estimate Eq. 5.5.[174] The results presented in Table 5.6 document that the coefficient of lagged STICKY is positively and statistically significant in both estimation methods providing evidence of the causal direction running from cost stickiness to expected cost of equity.

Table 5.6: Regression results lagging the main independent variable STICKY

Variable	Exp. sign	COE	
		OLS	Fama-MacBeth
L_STICKY	+	0.0025***	0.0018*
		(2.71)	(1.97)
BETA_R	+	0.0116***	0.0202***
		(5.92)	(3.88)
LOGSIZE_R	-	-0.0006	-0.0025
		(-1.08)	(-0.91)
BM_R	+	0.0029	0.0020
		(1.28)	(0.77)

174 Reverse causality refers to the direction of causality, i.e., risky firms could have incentives to maintain redundant resources. See Section 4.5 on p. 83 for details.

Table 5.6 continued

LEV_R	+	0.0619***	0.0554***
		(7.37)	(4.92)
ROA_R	+/-	-0.0659***	-0.0795***
		(-5.02)	(-2.90)
Constant	+/-	0.1438***	0.1552***
		(147.67)	(11.63)
N		18,188	18,188
Adjusted R^2		0.0110	0.0975

Table 5.6 presents the regression results for the lagged STICKY variable. The dependent variable is the expected cost of equity (COE) based on the Fama French Three Factor Model. The independent variables are L_STICKY and control variables as defined previously.

*(**, ***) Denotes significance at the 10% (5%, 1%) level (two-tailed). All continuous variables are winsorized at the 1% but COE between 0 and 1. The t-statistics in parentheses are calculated using robust standard errors clustered by the firm and year in OLS regression or is the Fama-MacBeth (1973) t-statistics.

5.4 Sensitivity Tests

For the purpose of checking the robustness of the results, I modify the sample with respect to estimated cost of equity and industry affiliation. Table 5.7 presents the results I obtain for each of the specifications.

5.4.1 More Extensive Data Trimming

In the main analysis I winsorize the estimated cost of equity between 0 and 1. To verify that my results do not suffer from the method to determine the outliers I apply two alternative approaches. First, rather than winsorize the negative and greater than one values I exclude them from my analysis. This procedure reduces the sample size by 12%, and the total number of observations decreases from 18,188 to 15,921. The results are reported in Table 5.7, Panel A. Further, Barth, Konchitchki, and Landsman (2013) trim their data more extensively, arguing that the cost of equity in excess of 50% is unlikely. Thus, I exclude the observations with cost of equity that are negative or greater than 50%. This outliers' treatment reduces the sample size by

14%, and the total number of observations decreases from 18,188 to 15,623. The results are shown in Table 5.7, Panel B. Both data trimming methods do not change my results qualitatively.

5.4.2 Industry Affiliation

As described in Section 5.2.1, I exclude firms from the financial or utility industries in my main analysis. As a further check for the robustness of my results I first repeat the analysis for all industries (Table 5.7, Panel C). Second, I follow Weiss (2010) and restrict the sample to industrial firms only (Table 5.7, Panel D). Reducing the sample to industrial firms has two advantages.[175] First, it provides a homogenous structure of the profit and loss statement among the firms. Second, industrial firms operate in competitive markets, thus restricting the sample to industrial firms mitigates the measurement error due to the changes in activity as a response to the changes in prices rather than volume.[176] Both industry specifications do not change my results qualitatively.

Table 5.7: Robustness analysis

Panel A: Excluding observations with estimated cost of equity less than 1 and exceeding 100%

Variable	Exp. sign	COE	
		OLS	Fama-MacBeth
STICKY	+	0.0037***	0.0037**
		(3.82)	(2.38)
BETA_R	+	0.0176***	0.0233***
		(8.66)	(5.10)
LOGSIZE_R	-	-0.0029***	-0.0050**
		(-5.00)	(-2.04)
BM_R	+	-0.0014	-0.0039
		(-0.62)	(-1.42)

175 See Weiss (2010), p. 1453.

176 The main disadvantage of restricting the sample to industrial firms is the reduced sample size which may lead to less variation in the independent STICKY variable and thus larger standard errors of the OLS estimator and therefore less accurate hypothesis tests (see Wooldridge 2012, p. 94).

Table 5.7 continued

LEV_R	+	0.0553***	0.0560***
		(6.61)	(4.85)
ROA_R	+/-	-0.0913***	-0.1076***
		(-6.81)	(-4.18)
Constant	+/-	0.1630***	0.1684***
		(164.11)	(12.90)
N		15,921	15,921
Adjusted R^2		0.0169	0.1043

Panel B: Excluding observations with estimated cost of equity less than 1 and exceeding 50%

		COE	
Variable	Exp. sign	OLS	Fama-MacBeth
STICKY	+	0.0029***	0.0037**
		(3.47)	(2.41)
BETA_R	+	0.0142***	0.0207***
		(7.86)	(5.50)
LOGSIZE_R	-	-0.0005	-0.0023
		(-0.88)	(-1.35)
BM_R	+	0.0003	-0.0022
		(0.17)	(-1.13)
LEV_R	+	0.0391***	0.0496***
		(5.40)	(4.59)
ROA_R	+/-	-0.0664***	-0.0668***
		(-5.70)	(-3.63)
Constant	+/-	0.1547***	0.1611***
		(175.41)	(13.80)
N		15,623	15,623
Adjusted R^2		0.0114	0.0921

Panel C: Including all industries

Variable	Exp. sign	COE	
		OLS	Fama-MacBeth
STICKY	+	0.0035***	0.0037**
		(4.58)	(2.69)
BETA_R	+	0.0221***	0.0286***
		(13.48)	(5.76)
LOGSIZE_R	-	0.0003	-0.0013
		(0.74)	(-0.50)
BM_R	+	0.0057***	0.0086***
		(2.92)	(3.72)
LEV_R	+	0.0234***	0.0138*
		(3.44)	(1.73)
ROA_R	+/-	-0.0700***	-0.0924***
		(-5.74)	(-3.32)
Constant	+/-	0.1395***	0.1530***
		(166.62)	(11.54)
N		23,627	23,627
Adjusted R^2		0.0133	0.1048

Panel D: Limiting to industrial firms

Variable	Exp. sign	COE	
		(1)	(2)
STICKY	+	0.0042***	0.0032*
		(3.57)	(1.88)
BETA_R	+	0.0111***	0.0218***
		(4.61)	(4.07)
LOGSIZE_R	-	-0.0005	-0.0034
		(-0.77)	(-1.23)

Table 5.7 continued

BM_R	+	0.0076**	0.0028
		(2.56)	(0.78)
LEV_R	+	0.0525***	0.0521***
		(4.73)	(3.81)
ROA_R	+/-	-0.0468***	-0.0816***
		(-2.95)	(-2.82)
Constant	+/-	0.1453***	0.1546***
		(118.23)	(11.22)
N		11,535	11,535
Adjusted R^2		0.0097	0.1055

Table 5.7 presents results of the effect of cost stickiness on the expected cost of equity.
Panel A reports the results when observations with negative values of expected cost of equity or values greater than 100% excluded.
Panel B shows the results when observations with negative values of expected cost of equity or values greater than 50% are excluded.
Panel C shows the results when firms belonging to financial and utility industries are included in the sample.
Panel D shows the results when the sample is restricted to industrial firms.
All variables as defined previously. *(**, ***) Denotes significance at the 10% (5%, 1%) level (two-tailed). The t-statistics in parentheses are calculated using robust standard errors clustered by the firm and year or is the Fama-MacBeth (1973) t-statistics.

Overall the results show that neither more extensive trimming of sample with respect to estimated cost of equity nor the industry affiliation change the conclusion that cost stickiness increases financial risk of a firm.

5.5 Summary and Conclusion

The aim of this chapter is to study the implications of asymmetric cost behavior for equity holders. For this purpose I examine the direct relation between cost stickiness and financial risk. Based on prior research I predict that asymmetric cost behavior increases riskiness of operating cash flows, resulting in the higher financial risk of a firm.

To test this hypothesis I estimate the expected cost of equity using the Fama French Three Factor Model and measure the degree of asymmetric cost behavior according to Weiss (2010). My analysis confirms the prediction of a positive association between cost stickiness and financial risk. The results are robust to alternative empirical specifications. My results are also robust to a specification in which I lag my main independent variable (STICKY) to reduce reverse causality concerns.

The documented finding of a positive association of cost asymmetry and expected cost of equity is of interest to managers, investors and analysts. Managers can benefit from the knowledge that maintaining redundant resources causes an increase in financial risk and the financing costs. Analysts and investors may take advantage of my results by better evaluating investments and performing corporate valuation.

6 Concluding Remarks, Limitations, and Future Research

This thesis investigated the cost stickiness phenomenon and provided two empirical studies of the consequences of asymmetric cost behavior on the credit and financial risk of a firm. In the following I summarize the results of my thesis before discussing its limitations and providing suggestions for future research.

6.1 Summary of Results

In Chapter 2 I provided the theoretical framework of cost stickiness concept in research and practice. First I introduced the origin and development of asymmetric cost behavior from the 1920s of the past century up until today. I further discussed the occurrence of cost stickiness in companies, thereby distinguishing between intended and unintended managerial decisions as well as providing a discussion of the main empirical models measuring the degree of cost stickiness. In addition I summarized empirical findings in the cost literature and classified them into three main groups: studies providing evidence on the existence of cost stickiness, studies analyzing the determinants of cost stickiness and, finally, studies examining the implications of asymmetric cost behavior.

In Chapter 3 I reviewed the credit risk fundamentals that were essential for the empirical study that followed. Thereby I demonstrated how credit risk could be measured based on theoretical models or deviated from the market prices of credit derivative instruments. I further discussed the development of the CDS market and presented an overview of the current research providing evidence on the superiority of CDS as a measure for credit risk over other credit derivative instruments. The main advantage of using the CDS as a measure for credit risk is that it does not contain components irrelevant to credit risk such as an illiquidity premium or taxes premium as is the case with bonds.

In the fourth chapter I presented an empirical study on the effect of asymmetric cost behavior on the credit risk of a firm. Thereby I measured the credit risk with CDSs, the most popular credit derivative instruments. The effect of cost stickiness on credit risk was not obvious at first view. I therefore elaborated three channels upon which asymmetric cost behavior might affect credit risk. According to the first channel, cost stickiness increases earnings volatility and therefore asset volatility, a key

K. Reimer, *Asymmetric Cost Behavior*, Quantitatives Controlling,
https://doi.org/10.1007/978-3-658-22822-4_6

determinant in pricing the credit risk. According to the second channel cost stickiness decreases the precision of accounting information, a proven determinant of credit risk. According to the third channel, cost stickiness increases future earnings and therefore the asset value of a firm. While the first two channels increase the credit risk, the latter decreases credit risk. My investigation of US firms in the time period from 2001 to 2011 demonstrated that firms with sticky cost behavior exhibit higher credit spreads. The results suggested that the first two channels prevail over the value enhancing channel and the overall effect of sticky costs is negative, that is, cost stickiness significantly increases a firm's credit risk when controlling for well-known credit risk determinants. The findings were shown to hold for CDS on both senior and subordinated debt of all maturities and be robust to different lag structures, variable measurement and alternative model specifications. Further, I demonstrated that the effect of cost stickiness increasing credit risk is lower for firms enjoying favorable conditions, operating in states with more operating flexibility.

In Chapter 5 I presented the second empirical study where I analyzed the effect of asymmetric cost behavior on the financial risk of equity. In line with my hypothesis that the equity holders expect a compensation for a higher risk bearing resulting from "investment" in excess resources, I documented that cost stickiness increases the expected cost of equity measured by the Fama French Three Factor Model. Further, the results suggested that the risk associated with sticky costs is correlated to a firm's fundamental characteristics, but also bears risk information beyond the known predictors of future returns in the Fama French Model.

6.2 Limitations and Propositions for Future Research

The investigations in this thesis offer a wide range of valuable insights to corporate insiders and outsiders alike, however it should be kept in mind that they are also subject to certain limitations, which in turn present a number of possibilities for future research.

The major limitation of Chapter 4 is the restricted sample in two dimensions. First, the data on CDS spreads are, to a larger extent, only available from 2001. The sample period covers 10 years in total, including the financial crisis of 2007. While the year fixed effects included in the regression analysis mitigates the concern that the credit spreads are affected by some omitted potential macro-economic factors, the analyzed period did not allow for the implementation of the difference-in-difference method in addition to the firm fixed effects approach to alleviate the endogeneity concern.[177] Right-to-work laws or wrongful-discharge laws could be possible exogenous shocks that should affect the level of cost stickiness. Second, the requirement of the availability of accounting and stock data results in a significant decrease in the number of analyzed companies, where CDS data were merged with accounting data. One third of the examined firms accounts to the financial industry. Although the results remain qualitatively unchanged when I exclude financials, this additional restriction makes any generalization of the results difficult.

Another caveat of the study presented in Chapter 4 concerns the fact that I did not differentiate between the sources of cost stickiness as it goes beyond the scope of this thesis. Previous literature has shown that apart from the economically driven resource-adjustment considerations, sticky costs may arise from irrational managerial decisions such as overconfidence and empire building incentives. The irrational drivers of cost stickiness should negatively affect future earnings, and thus the asset value resulting in even higher credit risk. Therefore differentiating between "good" and "bad" stickiness would be of benefit in predicting credit risk more precisely.

Similarly, in Chapter 5 I measured the average impact of cost stickiness on the expected cost of equity without differentiating between good and bad cost stickiness. While the good cost stickiness is capable of generating higher future earnings, the bad cost stickiness is a result of irrational decisions and/or incompetent management leading to lower earnings in the future. Thus, while cost stickiness leads to higher earnings volatility and less earnings persistence independent of the source of cost stickiness and therefore higher default and financial risk, the good cost stickiness should partially reduce the risk via its capability to generate higher future earnings and thus through the higher asset value. While I envisage a positive association between sticky costs and the expected cost of equity for bad and good cost stickiness, the risk premium for the firms with bad sticky costs should be higher than for the firms with good sticky costs. Further research could examine the differences in the amount of the cost of equity for good and bad sticky firms.

The main results of the two empirical studies demonstrate the consequences of cost stickiness on credit and financial risk. Yet, as shown by the previous literature and in the theoretical considerations of this thesis, cost stickiness also has a value enhancing implication. Thus a firm with a higher level of resources can satisfy demand in periods of activity increases and may therefore earn higher profits. Since

177 Difference-in-difference method calculates the effect of treatment of explanatory variable on dependent variable. Thereby the data from the same examination must be available for at least to points in time before and after the treatment.

a firm's value is equal to discounted future earnings and cost stickiness affects both the nominator (via future earnings) and the denominator (via higher cost of capital), the optimal level of cost stickiness remains an open question. This is therefore a fruitful point of departure for future research since investigating this issue would provide valuable insights to management and investors. Furthermore, the creditors do not participate fully on the upside risk and are concerned with the downside risk, while the firm's owners gain fully the potential profits less loan obligations. Consequently, the optimal level of cost stickiness should differ for equity and debt holders, where the optimal level for the debt holders should be significantly lower than for the equity holders.

Apart from my above suggestions for further research, the analysis of the cost stickiness literature also reveals the research gap in the drivers of cost stickiness. The theoretical considerations of the occurrence of unintended cost stickiness, which were presented in Chapter 2, had not previously been empirically analyzed.[178] Quantifying the cost stickiness that is unintended and concurrently unavoidable would provide a new angle on a firm's operational efficiency. Further, little is known about cost stickiness arising from rational managerial decisions that are not economically driven, i.e., those that do not have maximizing the value of the firm as their primary objective. This source of cost stickiness would probably be more relevant for non-profit organizations, such as government hospitals or educational institutions, but there is no doubt that a more extensive understanding of the drivers of cost stickiness would enrich the interpretation of its implications for various issues in financial and managerial accounting research.

178 One exception can be found in the study by Kama and Weiss (2010), which shows a mechanical driver of cost stickiness: previously established technological constraints result in unintended cost stickiness in the current period.

Appendix

Appendix 1: Derivation of d_1 in Merton model

It should be shown that d_1 defined in Black-Scholes formula (Eq. 3.4) is equivalent to d_1 defined in Merton formula (Eq. 3.7).

$$d_1 = \frac{1}{\sigma\sqrt{T-t}} \cdot \left[ln\left(\frac{V_t}{D}\right) + \left(r_f + \frac{1}{2}\sigma^2\right)(T-t)\right]$$

$$= \frac{1}{\sigma\sqrt{T-t}} \cdot \left[\ln\left(\frac{1}{L}\right) + \frac{1}{2}\sigma^2(T-t)\right]$$

Derivation

$$d_1 = \frac{1}{\sigma\sqrt{T-t}} \cdot \left[ln\left(\frac{V_t}{D}\right) + \left(r_f + \frac{1}{2}\sigma^2\right)(T-t)\right]$$

$$= \frac{1}{\sigma\sqrt{T-t}} \cdot \left[ln\left(\frac{V_t}{D}\right) + r_f(T-t) + \frac{1}{2}\sigma^2(T-t)\right]$$

$$= \frac{1}{\sigma\sqrt{T-t}} \cdot \left[ln\left(\frac{V_t}{D}\right) + ln(e^{r_f(T-t)}) + \frac{1}{2}\sigma^2(T-t)\right]$$

$$= \frac{1}{\sigma\sqrt{T-t}} \cdot \left[ln\left(\frac{V_t}{D}\right) + ln\left(\frac{1}{e^{-r_f(T-t)}}\right) + \frac{1}{2}\sigma^2(T-t)\right]$$

$$= \frac{1}{\sigma\sqrt{T-t}} \cdot \left[ln\left(\frac{V_t}{D \cdot e^{-r_f(T-t)}}\right) + \frac{1}{2}\sigma^2(T-t)\right]$$

$$= \frac{1}{\sigma\sqrt{T-t}} \cdot \left[ln(V_t) - ln(D \cdot e^{-r_f(T-t)}) + \frac{1}{2}\sigma^2(T-t)\right]$$

$$= \frac{1}{\sigma\sqrt{T-t}} \cdot \left[-[\ln(D \cdot e^{-r_f(T-t)}) - ln(V_t)] + \frac{1}{2}\sigma^2 \cdot (T-t)\right]$$

$$= \frac{1}{\sigma\sqrt{T-t}} \cdot \left[-ln\left(\frac{D \cdot e^{-r_f(T-t)}}{V_t}\right) + \frac{1}{2}\sigma^2(T-t)\right]$$

with $\quad L = \frac{D \cdot e^{-r_f(T-t)}}{V_t}$

$$= \frac{1}{\sigma\sqrt{T-t}} \cdot \left[ln\left(\frac{1}{L}\right) + \frac{1}{2}\sigma^2(T-t)\right]$$

K. Reimer, *Asymmetric Cost Behavior*, Quantitatives Controlling,
https://doi.org/10.1007/978-3-658-22822-4

Appendix 2: Derivation of d_2 in Merton model

It should be shown that d_2 defined in Black-Scholes formula (Eq. 3.5) is equivalent to d_2 defined in Merton formula (Eq. 3.8).

$$d_2 = d_1 - \sigma\sqrt{T-t} = \frac{ln\left(\frac{1}{L}\right) - \frac{1}{2}\sigma^2(T-t)}{\sigma\sqrt{T-t}}$$

Derivation

$$d_2 = d_1 - \sigma\sqrt{T-t}$$

$$\text{with } d_1 = \frac{1}{\sigma\sqrt{T-t}} \cdot \left[ln\left(\frac{1}{L}\right) + \frac{1}{2}\sigma^2(T-t)\right]$$

$$= \frac{1}{\sigma\sqrt{T-t}} \cdot \left[\ln\left(\frac{1}{L}\right) + \frac{1}{2}\sigma^2(T-t)\right] - \sigma\sqrt{T-t}$$

$$= \frac{1}{\sigma\sqrt{T-t}} \cdot \left[\ln\left(\frac{1}{L}\right) + \frac{1}{2}\sigma^2(T-t) - \sigma^2(T-t)\right]$$

$$= \frac{1}{\sigma\sqrt{T-t}} \cdot \left[ln\left(\frac{1}{L}\right) - \frac{1}{2}\sigma^2(T-t)\right]$$

Appendix 3: Derivation of Merton's credit spread

It should be shown that credit spread, defined as difference between yield to maturity and riskless rate $(r^* - r_f)$ is equal to $-\frac{1}{(T-t)} \cdot ln\left[N(d_2) + \frac{1}{L} \cdot N(-d_1)\right]$ with yield to maturity defined in Eq. 3.11:

$r^* = -\frac{1}{(T-t)} \cdot \left[ln\left(\frac{e^{-r_f(T-t)} \cdot D - P}{D}\right)\right]$.

Derivation

$$r^* - r_f = -\frac{1}{(T-t)} \cdot \left[ln\left(\frac{e^{-r_f(T-t)} \cdot D - P}{D}\right)\right] - r_f$$

$$= -\frac{1}{(T-t)} \cdot \left[ln\left(\frac{e^{-r_f(T-t)} \cdot D - P}{D}\right) + r_f(T-t)\right]$$

$$with\ P = e^{-r_f(T-t)} \cdot D \cdot N(-d_2) - V_t \cdot N(-d_1)$$

$$= -\frac{1}{(T-t)} \cdot \left[ln\left(\frac{e^{-r_f(T-t)} \cdot D - e^{-r_f(T-t)} \cdot D \cdot N(-d_2) + V_t \cdot N(-d_1)}{D}\right) + \ln(e^{r_f(T-t)})\right]$$

$$= -\frac{1}{(T-t)} \cdot ln\left[\frac{e^{r_f(T-t)}(e^{-r_f(T-t)} \cdot D - e^{-r_f(T-t)} \cdot D \cdot N(-d_2) + V_t \cdot N(-d_1))}{D}\right]$$

$$= -\frac{1}{(T-t)} \cdot ln\left[\frac{D - D \cdot N(-d_2) + V_t \cdot e^{r_f(T-t)} \cdot N(-d_1)}{D}\right]$$

$$= -\frac{1}{(T-t)} \cdot ln\left[1 - N(-d_2) + \frac{V_t \cdot N(-d_1)}{e^{-r_f(T-t)} \cdot D}\right]$$

$$with\ L = \frac{e^{-r_f(T-t)} \cdot D}{V_t}$$

$$= -\frac{1}{(T-t)} \cdot ln\left[N(d_2) + \frac{1}{L} \cdot N(-d_1)\right]$$

Appendix 4

Table A.1 shows the panel data regression results of the standardized impact of cost stickiness on credit risk based on the main sample for 5-year CDS contracts.

Table A.1: Standardized impact of cost stickiness on credit risk

Based on the sample covering only 5-year CDS contracts		
Variable	Exp. sign	SPREAD
STICKY	+	26.7830***
		(3.86)
LEV	+	21.4902
		(0.59)
RF	-	-42.5224
		(-1.60)
VOL	+	52.0103***
		(3.66)
SENIORITY	-	-42.8650***
		(-2.99)
CUMR	+	20.8872***
		(3.94)
EXR	-	-3.3314
		(-0.51)
SIZE	-	-332.5729***
		(-3.75)
ROA	-	-4.7640
		(-0.42)
Constant	+/-	-7.9464
		(-0.10)
N		2,906
Number of firms		130
Firm FE		YES
Year FE		YES

Adjusted R^2	0.3576

*(**, ***) Denotes significance at the 10% (5%, 1%) level (two-tailed). All continuous variables are trimmed at the 0.5%. The t-statistics in parentheses are calculated using robust standard errors clustered by the firm. In this table, every given firm is represented as many times as CDS spreads are available for that company. The dependent variable (SPREAD) is CDS premium measured in basis points one working day after the SEC filing. The independent variables are as defined in Table 4.2, on p. 78. All independent continuous variables are standardized.

Appendix 5

Table A.2 presents the results of the effect of sticky dummy on 5-year CDS spreads measured in basis points.

Table A.2: Impact of cost stickiness on credit risk measured with CDS premia in basis points

Based on the sample covering only 5-year CDS contracts		
Variable	Exp. sign	SPREAD
D_STICKY	+	37.9883***
		(3.06)
LEV	+	172.4312
		(0.76)
RF	-	-24.6383
		(-1.59)
VOL	+	4,920.3408***
		(3.64)
SENIORITY	-	-43.3367***
		(-3.06)
CUMR	+	21.3460***
		(3.97)
EXR	-	-3.3878
		(-0.51)
SIZE	-	-226.3481***
		(-3.67)
ROA	-	12.6674
		(0.01)
Constant	+/-	41.4660
		(0.46)
N		2,906
Number of firms		130
Firm FE		YES

Year FE	YES
Adjusted R^2	0.3518

*(**, ***) Denotes significance at the 10% (5%, 1%) level (two-tailed). All continuous variables are trimmed at the 0.5%. The t-statistics in parentheses are calculated using robust standard errors clustered by the firm. In this table, every given firm is represented as many times as CDS spreads are available for that company. The dependent variable (SPREAD) is CDS premium measured in basis points one working day after the SEC filing. The independent variables are D_STICKY, an indicator variable equal to 1 when a firm exhibits sticky cost behavior and 0 otherwise. All other variables are as defined in Table 4.2, on p. 78.

References

Abarbanell, J. S., W. N. Lanen, and E. R. Verrecchia. 1995. Analysts' forecasts as proxies for investor beliefs in empirical research. *Journal of Accounting and Economics* 20 (1): 31-60.

Abu-Serdaneh, J. 2014. The Asymmetrical Behavior of Cost: Evidence from Jordan. *International Business Research* 7 (8): 113-122.

Acharya, V. V., and T. C. Johnson. 2007. Insider trading in credit derivatives. *Journal of Financial Economics* 84 (1): 110-141.

Altman, E. I., A. Resti, and A. Sironi. 2004. Default Recovery Rates in Credit Risk Modeling: A Review of the Literature and Empirical Evidence. *Economic Notes* 33 (2): 183-208.

Anderson, M. C., R. D. Banker, and S. N. Janakiraman. 2003. Are Selling, General, and Administrative Costs "Sticky"? *Journal of Accounting Research* 41 (1): 47-63.

Anderson, M. C., R. D. Banker, R. Huang, and S. N. Janakiraman. 2007. Cost Behavior and Fundamental Analysis of SG&A Costs. *Journal of Accounting, Auditing & Finance* 22 (1): 1-28.

Anderson, S. W. and W. N. Lanen. 2009. *Understanding Cost Management: What Can We Learn from the Evidence on 'Sticky Costs'?* Working Paper, Rice University and University of Michigan.

Argilés, J. M. and J. García-Blandón. 2009. Cost stickiness revisited: empirical application for farms. *Spanish Journal of Finance an Accounting* 38 (144): 579-605.

Arora, N., P. Gandhi, and F. A. Longstaff. 2012. Counterparty credit risk and the credit default swap market. *Journal of Financial Economics* 103 (2): 280-293.

K. Reimer, *Asymmetric Cost Behavior*, Quantitatives Controlling,
https://doi.org/10.1007/978-3-658-22822-4

Arora, N., S. Richardson, and İ. Tuna. 2014. Asset reliability and security prices: evidence from credit markets. *Review of Accounting Studies* 19 (1): 363-395.

Augustin, P., M. G. Subrahmanyam, D. Y. Tang, and S. Q. Wang. 2014. Credit default swaps: A survey. *Foundations and Trends in Finance* 9 (1-2): 1-196.

Balakrishnan, R. and T. Gruca. 2008. Cost stickiness and core competency: A note. *Contemporary Accounting Research* 25 (4): 993-1006.

Balakrishnan, R., M. J. Petersen, and N. S. Soderstrom. 2004. Does Capacity Utilization Affect the "Stickiness" of Cost? *Journal of Accounting, Auditing & Finance* 19 (3): 283-299.

Balakrishnan,R., E. Labro, and N. S. Soderstrom. 2014. Cost Structure and Sticky Costs. *Journal of Management Accounting Research* 26 (2): 91-116.

Banker, R. D. and D. Byzalov. 2014. Asymmetric Cost Behavior. *Journal of Management Accounting Research* 26 (2): 43-79.

Banker, R. D. and L. Chen. 2006a. *Labor Market Characteristics and Cross-Country Differences in Cost Stickiness.* Working Paper, Temple University, Georgia State University.

Banker, R. D. and L. Chen. 2006b. Predicting Earnings Using a Model Based on Cost Variability and Cost Stickiness. *The Accounting Review* 81 (2): 285-307.

Banker, R. D. and S. Fang. 2013. *Loan Financing and Real Cost Management.* Working Paper, Temple University.

Banker, R. D., D. Byzalov, and J. M. Plehn-Dujowich. 2011. *Sticky Cost Behavior: Theory and Evidence.* Working Paper, Temple University.

Banker, R. D., D. Byzalov, and J. M. Plehn-Dujowich. 2014. Demand Uncertainty and Cost Behavior. *The Accounting Review* 89 (3): 839-865.

Banker, R. D., D. Byzalov, and L. Chen. 2013. Employment protection legislation, adjustment costs and cross-country differences in cost behavior. *Journal of Accounting and Economics* 55 (1): 111-127.

Banker, R. D., D. Byzalov, and L. Threinen. 2013. *Determinants of International Differences in Asymmetric Cost Behavior.* Working Paper, Temple University - Fox School of Business.

Banker, R. D., D. Byzalov, M. Ciftci, and R. Mashruwala. 2014. The Moderating Effect of Prior Sales Changes on Asymmetric Cost Behavior. *Journal of Management Accounting Research* 26 (2): 221-242.

Banker, R. D., R. Flasher, and D. Zhang. 2014. *Strategic positioning and asymmetric cost behavior.* Working paper, Temple University.

Barth, M., Y. Konchitchki, and W. Landsman. 2013. Cost of capital and earnings transparency. *Journal of Accounting and Economics* 55 (2-3): 206-224.

Baumgarten, D., U. Bonenkamp, and C. Homburg. 2010. The Information Content of the SG&A Ratio. *Journal of Management Accounting Research* 22 (1): 1-22.

Benkert, C. 2004. Explaining Credit Default Swap Premia. *Journal of Futures Markets* 24 (1): 71-92.

Berndt, A., R. A. Jarrow, and C. Kang. 2007. Restructuring Risk in Credit Default Swaps: An Empirical Analysis. *Stochastic Processes and their Applications* 117 (11): 1724-1749.

Berndt, A., R. Douglas, D. Duffie, M. Ferguson and D. Schranz. 2005. *Measuring default risk premia from default swap rates and EDFs*. Working Paper, Bank for International Settlement.

Bernstein, L. A. 1988. *Financial Statement Analysis: Theory, Application, and Interpretation. 4th edition*. Homewood: Irwin.

Bhat, G., J. L. Callen, and D. Segal. 2014. Credit Risk and IFRS: The Case of Credit Default Swaps. *Journal of Accounting, Auditing & Finance* 29 (2): 129-162.

Bierman, H. and J. E. Hass. 1975. An analytical model of bond risk differentials. *Journal of Financial and Quantitative Analysis* 10 (5): 757-773.

BIS - Bank for International Settlements. 2007. Triennial Central Bank Survey: Foreign exchange and derivatives market activity in 2007. http://www.bis.org/publ/rpfxf07t.pdf. [Accessed 27.16.2017].

BIS - Bank for International Settlements. 2015. Triennial Central Bank Survey of Foreign Exchange and OTC Derivatives Market Activity. http://www.bis.org/statistics/triennialrep/2016survey_guidelinesoutstanding.pdf. [Accessed 27.06.2017].

BIS - Bank for International Settlements. 2016. OTC derivatives statistics at end-June-2016. http://www.bis.org/publ/otc_hy1611.pdf. [Accessed 23.11.2016].

Black, F. and M. Scholes. 1973. The pricing of options and corporate liabilities. *Journal of Political Economy* 81(3): 637-654.

Blanco, R., S. Brennan, and I. W. Marsh. 2005. An Empirical Analysis of the Dynamic Relation between Investment-Grade Bonds and Credit Default Swaps. *Journal of Finance* 60 (5): 2255-2281.

Bonenkamp, U., C. Homburg, and A. Kempf. 2011. Fundamental Information in Technical Trading Strategies. *Journal of Business Finance & Accounting* 38 (7-8): 842-860.

Bongaerts, D., F. De Jong, and J. Driessen. 2011. Derivative Pricing with Liquidity Risk: Theory and Evidence from the Credit Default Swap Market. *Journal of Finance* 66 (1): 203-240.

Bradbury, M. E and T. Scott. 2015. *Do managers understand asymmetrical cost behaviour?* Working Paper, Massey University, University of Auckland.

Brasch, H. D. 1927. Zur Praxis der Unkostenschwankungen und ihrer Erfassung. *Betriebswirtschaftliche Rundschau* 4 (4-5): 65-73.

Bu, D., C. Wen, and R. D. Banker. 2015. Implications of asymmetric cost behavior for analyzing financial reports of companies in China. *China Journal of Accounting Studies* 3 (3): 181-208.

Bugeja, M., M. Lu, and Y. Shan. 2015. Cost stickiness in Australia: Characteristics and Determinants. *Australian Accounting Review* 25 (3): 248-261.

Calleja, K., M. Steliaros, and D. C. Thomas. 2006. A Note on Cost Stickiness: Some International Comparisons. *Management Accounting Research* 17 (2): 127-140.

Callen, J. L., J. Livnat, and D. Segal. 2009. The Impact of Earnings on the Pricing of Credit Default Swaps. *The Accounting Review* 84 (5): 1363-1394.

Campbell, J. Y. and G. B. Taksler. 2003. Equity Volatility and Corporate Bond Yields. *Journal of Finance* 58 (6): 2321-2350.

Campbell, T. C., D. C. Chichernea, and A. Petkevich. 2016. Dissecting the bond profitability premium. *Journal of Financial Markets* 27: 102-131.

Cannon, J. N. 2014. Determinants of "Sticky Costs": An Analysis of Cost Behavior using United States Air Transportation Industry Data. *The Accounting Review* 89 (5): 1645-1672.

Chen, C. X., H. Lu, and T. Sougiannis. 2012. The Agency Problem, Corporate Governance, and the Asymmetrical Behavior of Selling, General, and Administrative Costs. *Contemporary Accounting Research* 29 (1): 252-282.

Chen, C. X., T. Gores, and J. Nasev. 2013. *Managerial Overconfidence and Cost Stickiness*. Working Paper, University of Illinois at Urbana-Champaign, University of Cologne.

Chen, E. H., and W. J. Dixon. 1972. Estimates of Parameters of a Censored Regression Sample. *Journal of the American Statistical Association* 67 (339): 664-671.

Chen, H. J., M. Kacperczyk, and H. Ortiz-Molina. 2011. Labor Unions, Operating Flexibility, and the Cost of Equity. *Journal of Financial and Quantitative Analysis* 46 (1): 25-58.

Chen, L., R. Novy-Marx, and L. Zhang. 2011. *An Alternative Three-Factor Model*. Working Paper, Washington University in St. Louis, University of Rochester, Ohio State University.

Chen, T. K., H. H. Liao, and W. L. Chen. 2014. Production efficiency uncertainty and corporate credit risk: Structural form credit model perspectives. *Journal of Empirical Finance* 29 (December): 266-280.

Chen, T. K., Y. Tseng, and Y. T. Hsieh. 2015. Real Earnings Management Uncertainty and Corporate Credit Risk. *European Accounting Review* 24 (3): 413-440.

Chiu, T.-T., Y. Guan, and J.-B. Kim. 2015. *The Effect of Risk Factor Disclosures on the Pricing of Credit Default Swaps*. Working Paper, Norwegian School of Economics, City University of Hong Kong, University of Waterloo.

Ciftci, M., R. Mashruwala, and D. Weiss. 2016. Implications of Cost Behavior for Analysts' Earnings Forecasts. *Journal of Management Accounting Research* 28 (1): 57-80.

Collin-Dufresne, P., R. S. Goldstein, and J. S. Martin. 2001. The Determinants of Credit Spread Changes. *Journal of Finance* 56 (6): 2177-2207.

Cooper, R. and J. Haltiwanger. 2006. On the nature of capital adjustment costs. *Review of Economic Studies* 73 (3): 611-633.

Cooper, R. and R. S. Kaplan. 1988. How Cost Accounting Distorts Product Costs. *Management Accounting* 69 (10): 20-27.

Correia, M., J. Kang, and S. Richardson. 2015. *Does Fundamental Volatility Help Explain Credit Risk?* Working Paper, London Business School, BlackRock, AQR Capital Management LLC.

Correia, M., S. Richardson, and İ. Tuna. 2012. Value investing in credit markets. *Review of Accounting Studies* 17 (3): 572-609.

Crouhy, M., D. Galai, and R. Mark. 2001. *Risk Management*. New York, NY: McGraw-Hill.

Das, S. R., P. Hanouna, and A. Sarin. 2009. Accounting-based versus market-based cross-sectional models of CDS spreads. *Journal of Banking & Finance* 33 (4): 719-730.

De Medeiros, O. R. and P. de Souza Costa. 2004. *Cost Stickiness in Brazilian Firms*. Working Paper, University of Brasilia.

Dichev, I. D. and V. W. Tang. 2009. Earnings volatility and earnings predictability. *Journal of Accounting and Economics* 47 (1-2): 160-181.

Dierynck, B., W. R. Landsman, and A. Renders. 2012. Do Managerial Incentives Drive Cost Behavior? Evidence about the Role of the Zero Earnings Benchmark for Labor Cost Behavior in Private Belgian Firms. *The Accounting Review* 87 (4): 1219-1246.

Douglas, A. V. S., A. G. Huang, and K. R. Vetzal. 2014. Cash flow volatility and corporate bond yield spreads. *Review of Quantitative Finance and Accounting* 46 (2): 417-458.

Duffie, D. 1999. Credit swap valuation. *Financial Analysts Journal* 55 (1): 73-87.

Duffie, D. and D. Lando. 2001. Term Structures of Credit Spreads with Incomplete Accounting Information. *Econometrica* 69 (3): 633-664.

Duffie, D. and K. J. Singleton. 1999. Modeling the Term Structures of Defaultable Bonds. *Review of Financial Studies* 12 (4): 687-720.

Duffie, D. and K. J. Singleton. 2003. *Credit Risk: Pricing, Measurement, and Management.* Princeton and Oxford: Princeton University Press.

Duffie, D., A. Li, and T. Lubke. 2010. Policy Perspectives on OTC Derivatives Market Infrastructure. Federal Reserve Bank of New York. http://www.iaqf.org/dev/files/sr424_duffie%20paper.pdf . [Accessed 26.06.2017].

Easton, P. D., S. J. Monahan, and F. P. Vasvari. 2009. Initial Evidence on the Role of Accounting Earnings in the Bond Market. *Journal of Accounting Research* 47 (3): 721-766.

Elton, E. J., M. J. Gruber, D. Agrawal, and C. Mann. 2001. Explaining the rate spread on corporate bonds. *Journal of Finance* 56 (1): 247-277.

Engle, R. and C. Granger. 1987. Co-integration and Error Correction: Representation, Estimation, and Testing. *Econometrica* 55 (2): 251-276.

Eom, Y. H., J. Helwege, and J. Z. Huang. 2004. Structrual Models of Corporate Bond Pricing: An Empirical Analysis. *Review of Financial Studies* 17 (2): 499-544.

Ericsson, J., K. Jacobs, and R. Oviedo. 2009. The Determinants of Credit Default Swap Premia. *Journal of Financial and Quantitative Analysis* 44 (1): 109-132.

Fairfield, P., R. Sweeney, and T. Yohn. 1996. Accounting classification and the predictive content of earnings. *The Accounting Review* 71 (3): 337-355.

Fama, E. and K. French. 1995. Size and Book-to-Market Factor in Earnings and Returns. *Journal of Finance* 50 (1): 131-155.

Fama, E. F. and J.D. MacBeth. 1973. Risk, Return, and Equilibrium: Empirical Tests. *Journal of Political Economy* 81 (3): 607-636.

Fama, E. F. and K. R French. 1993. Common risk factors in the returns on stocks and bonds. *Journal of Financial Economics* 33 (1): 3-56.

Fama, E. F. and K. R French. 2006. Profitability, investment and average returns. *Journal of Financial Economics* 82 (3): 491-518.

Fama, E. F. and K. R French. 2008. Dissecting anomalies. *Journal of Finance* 63 (4): 1653-1678.

Fama, E. F. and K. R French. 2015. A five-factor asset pricing model. *Journal of Financial Economics* 116 (1): 1-22.

Francis, J., R. LaFond, P. Olsson, and K. Schipper. 2005. The market pricing of accruals quality. *Journal of Accounting and Economics* 39 (2): 295-327.

Galai, D., and R. W. Masulis. 1976. The Option Pricing Model and the Risk Factor of Stock. *Journal of Financial Economics* 3 (January-March): 53-81.

Garrison, R. H., E. W. Noreen, and P. C. Brewer. 2015. *Managerial Accounting. 15th edition.* New York, NY: McGraw-Hill.

Garvin, J. L. (editor). 1929. *The Encyclopaedia Britannica: A New Survey of Universal Knowledge. 14th edition, Vol. 19.* London: The Encyclopaedia Britannica Co.

Gehde-Trapp, M., Y. Gündüz, and J. Nasev. 2015. The Liquidity Premium in CDS Transaction Prices: Do Frictions Matter? *Journal of Banking & Finance* 61 (December): 184-205.

Geske, R. 1977. The Valuation of Corporate Liabilities as Compound Options. *Journal of Financial and Quantitative Analysis* 12 (4): 63-81.

Geske, R. 1979. The Valuation of Compound Options. *Journal of Financial Economics* 7 (March): 63-81.

Gkougkousi, X. 2014. Aggregate Earnings and Corporate Bond Markets. *Journal of Accounting Research* 52 (1): 75-106.

Goldstein, R., N. Ju, and H. Leland. 2001. An EBIT-Based Model of Dynamic Capital Structure. *The Journal of Business* 74 (4): 483-512.

Gonzalo, J. and C. W. J. Granger. 1995. Estimation of common long-memory components in cointegrated systems. *Journal of Business & Economic Statistics* 13 (1): 27-36.

Goux D., E. Maurin, and M. Pauchet. 2001. Fixed-term contracts and the dynamics of labour demand. *European Economic Review* 45 (3): 533-552.

Granger, C. W. 1981. Some properties of time series data and their use in econometric model specification. *Journal of Econometrics* 16 (1): 121-130.

Griffin, P. A. 2014. The market for credit default swaps: new insights into investors' use of accounting information? *Accounting and Finance* 54 (3): 847-883.

Griffin, P. A., H. A. Hong, J.-B. Kim, and J.-H. Lim. 2015. *The SEC's XBRL Mandate and Credit Risk: Evidence on a Link between Credit Default Swap Pricing and XBRL Disclosure*. Working Paper, University of California, City University of Hong Kong, University of Waterloo.

Guenther, T. W., A. Riehl, and R. Rößler. 2014. Cost stickiness: state of the art of research and implications. *Journal of Management Control* 24 (4): 301-318.

Gündüz, Y. and M. Uhrig-Homburg. 2014. Does modeling framework matter? A comparative study of structural and reduced-form models. *Review of Derivatives Research* 17 (1): 39-78.

Güntay, L. and D. Hackbarth. 2010. Corporate bond credit spreads and forecast dispersion. *Journal of Banking & Finance* 34 (10): 2328-2345.

Hann, R. N., F. Heflin, and K. R. Subramanayam. 2007. Fair-value pension accounting. *Journal of Accounting and Economics* 44 (3): 328-358.

Hasbrouck, J. 1995. One security, many markets: Determining the contributions to price discovery, *Journal of Finance* 50 (4): 1175-1199.

Hasenack W. 1925. Betriebskalkulationen im Bankgewerbe. Bank- und finanzwirtschaftliche Abhandlungen. Springer.

He, D. S., J. Teruya, and T. Shimizu. 2010. Sticky Selling, General, and Administrative Cost Behavior and its Changes in Japan. *Global Journal of Business Research* 4 (4): 1-10.

Homburg, C., J. Nasev, K. Reimer, and M. Uhrig-Homburg. 2016. *Does Cost Management Affect Credit Risk?* Working Paper, University of Cologne, Karlsruhe Institute of Technology (KIT) - Institute for Finance.

Horngren, C. T., S. M. Datar, and M. V. Rajan. 2015. *Cost Accounting: A Managerial Emphasis. 15th edition.* Upper Saddle River, NJ : Pearson.

Houweling, P. and T. Vorst. 2005. Pricing Default Swaps: Empirical Evidence. *Journal of International Money and Finance* 24 (8): 1200-1225.

Hull, J. H. 2006. *Options, Futures, and Other Derivatives. 6th edition.* New Jersey: Person Prentice Hall.

Ibrahim, A. E. A. 2015. Economic growth and cost stickiness: Evidence from Egypt. *Journal of Financial Reporting and Accounting* 13 (1): 119-140.

ISDA- International Swaps & Derivatives Association. 2008. The ISDA Market Survey: What the results show and what they don't show. *ISDA Research Notes. http://www.isda.org/researchnotes/pdf/researchnotes-Autumn2008.pdf.* [Accessed 27.11.2016].

Jaramillo, F., F. Schiantarelli, and A. Sembenelli. 1993. Are adjustment costs for labor asymmetric? An econometric test on panel data for Italy. *Review of Economics and Statistics* 75 (4): 640-648.

Jarrow, R. A. 2011. Credit market equilibrium theory and evidence: Revisiting the structural versus reduced form credit risk model debate. *Finance Research Letters* 8 (1): 2-7.

Jarrow, R. A. and S. Turnbull. 1995. Pricing Derivatives on Financial Securities Subject to Credit Risk. *Journal of Finance* 50 (1): 53-85.

Jarrow, R. A., D. Lando, and S. M. Turnbull. 1997. A Markov Model for the Term Structure of Credit Spreads. *Review of Financial Studies* 10 (2): 481-523.

Jarrow, R., H. Li, S. Liu, and C.Wu. 2010. Reduced form valuation of callable corporate bonds: theory and evidence. *Journal of Financial Economics* 95 (2): 227-248.

Jensen, M. C. 1986. Agency costs of free cash flow, corporate finance, and takeovers. *American Economic Review* 76 (3): 323-329.

Jensen, M. C. and W. H. Meckling. 1976. Theory of the Firm: Managerial Behavior, Agency Costs and Ownership Structure. *Journal of Financial Economics* 3 (4): 305-360.

Jonkart, M., 1979. On the term structure of interest rate and the risk of default: an analytical approach. *Journal of Banking and Finance* 3 (3): 253-262.

Jorion, P. and G. Zhang. 2007. Good and bad credit contagion: Evidence from credit default swaps. *Journal of Financial Economics* 84 (3): 860-883.

Jorion, P. and G. Zhang. 2009. Credit Contagion from Counterparty Risk. *Journal of Finance* 64 (5): 2053-2087.

Jung, B., N. S. Soderstrom, and Y. S. Yang. 2013. Earnings Smoothing Activities of Firms to Manage Credit Ratings. *Contemporary Accounting Research* 30 (2): 645-676.

Kama, I and D. Weiss. 2010. *Do Managers' Deliberate Decisions Induce Sticky Costs?* Working Paper, Tel Aviv University.

Kama, I. and D. Weiss. 2013. Do Earnings Targets and Managerial Incentives Affect Sticky Costs? *Journal of Accounting Research* 51 (1): 201-224.

Karpoff J. M., D. S. Lee, and G. S. Martin. 2008. The Cost to Firms of Cooking the Books. *Journal of Financial and Quantitative Analysis* 43 (3): 581-612.

Kim, S., P. Kraft, and S. G. Ryan. 2013. Financial statement comparability and credit risk. *Review of Accounting Studies* 18 (3): 783-823.

Kraft, P. 2015. Rating Agency Adjustments to GAAP Financial Statements and Their Effect on Ratings and Credit Spreads. *The Accounting Review* 90 (2): 641-674.

Krishnan, R. 2015. Management Accountant-What Ails Thee? *Journal of Management Accounting Research* 27 (1): 177-191.

Lando, D. 1998. On Cox Processes and Credit Risky Securities. *Review of Derivatives Research* 2 (2): 99-120.

Lee, S. Y. 2015. Cost behavior during the global financial crisis: The case of Korean commercial banks. *Asia-Pacific Journal of Multimedia Services Convergent with Art, Humanities, and Sociology* 5 (2): 387-394.

Leland, H. and K. B. Toft. 1996. Optimal Capital Structure, Endogenous Bankruptcy, and the Term Structure of Credit Spreads. *Journal of Finance* 51 (3): 987-1019.

Lev, B. and R. Thiagarajan. 1993. Fundamental Information Analysis. *Journal of Accounting Research* 31 (2): 190-215.

Lin, H., S. Liu, and C. Wu. 2011. Dissecting Corporate Bond and CDS spreads. *Journal of Fixed Income* 20 (3): 7-39.

Longstaff, F. A. and E. S. Schwartz. 1995. A simple approach to valuing risky fixed and floating rate debt. *Journal of Finance* 50 (3): 789-819.

Longstaff, F. A., S. Mithal, and E. Neis. 2005. Corporate Yield Spreads: Default Risk or Liquidity? New Evidence from the Credit Default Swap Market. *Journal of Finance* 60 (5): 2213-2253.

Longstaff, F. and A. Rajan. 2008. An empirical analysis of the pricing of collateralized debt obligations. *Journal of Finance* 63 (2): 529-563.

Mahlendorf, M. 2009. Sticky Cost Issues - Kostenremanenz bei Nachfrageschwankungen. *Controlling and Management* 53 (3): 193-195.

Malagoli, M. 1985. Probleme der Kostenremanenz in Theorie und Praxis, Kritik und Ergänzung. *Dissertation.* University of St. Gallen.

Markit. 2008. Markit Credit Indices: A Primer. https://www.markit.com/news/Credit%20Indices%20Primer.pdf. [Accessed 23.11.2016].

Mayordomo, S., J. I. Peña, and E. S. Schwartz. 2014. Are All Credit Default Swap Databases Equal? *European Financial Management* 20 (4): 677-713.

Merton, R. C. 1974. On the Pricing of Corporate Debt: The Risk Structure of Interest Rates. *Journal of Finance* 29 (2): 449-470.

Minton, B. A. and C. Schrand. 1999. The impact of cash flow volatility on discretionary investment and the costs of debt and equity financing. *Journal of Financial Economics* 54 (3): 423-460.

Molina, C. A. 2005. Are Firms Underleveraged? An Examination of the Effect of Leverage on Default Probabilities. *Journal of Finance* 60 (3): 1427-1459.

Nielsen, L. T. 1993. Understanding $N(d_1)$ and $N(d_2)$: Risk-adjusted probabilities in the Black-Scholes model. *Finance* 14 (1): 95-106.

Norden, L. and M. Weber. 2004. Informational efficiency of credit default swap and stock markets: The impact of credit rating announcements. *Journal of Banking and Finance* 28 (11): 2813-2843.

Noreen, E. 1991. Conditions under which Activity-Based Cost Systems Provide Relevant Costs. *Journal of Management Accounting Research* 3: 159-168.

Noreen, E. and N. Soderstrom. 1994. Are overhead costs strictly proportional to activity? Evidence from hospital departments. *Journal of Accounting and Economics* 17 (1): 255-278.

Noreen, E. and N. Soderstrom. 1997. The accuracy of proportional cost models: Evidence from hospital service departments. *Review of Accounting Studies* 2 (1): 89-114.

Novy-Marx, R., 2013. The other side of value: The gross profitability premium. *Journal of Financial Economics* 108 (1): 1-28.

Packer, F. and H. Zhu. 2005. Contractual terms and CDS pricing. *BIS Quarterly Review* (March): 89-100.

Pan, J. and K. J. Singleton. 2008. Default and recovery implicit in the term structure of sovereign CDS spreads. *Journal of Finance* 63 (5): 2345-2384.

Pastor, L., and P. Veronesi. 2003. Stock Valuation and Learning about Profitability. *Journal of Finance* 58 (5): 1749-1789.

Petersen, M. A. 2009. Estimating Standard Errors in Finance Panel Data Sets: Comparing Approaches. *The Review of Financial Studies* 22 (1): 435-480.

Porporato, M. and E. Werbin. 2012. Evidence of sticky costs in banks of Argentina, Brazil and Canada. *International Journal of Financial Services Management* 5 (4): 303-320.

Qin, B., A. W. Mohan, and Y. F. Kuang. 2015. CEO overconfidence and cost stickiness. *Management Control & Accounting* (2): 26-32.

Qiu, J. and F. Yu. 2012. Endogenous liquidity in credit derivatives. *Journal of Financial Economics* 103 (3): 611-631.

Resti, A. and A. Sironi. 2007. *Risk Management and Shareholders' Value in Banking. From Risk Measurement Models to Capital Allocation Policies*. Chichester: John Wiley & Sons Ltd.

Rouxelin, F., W. Wongsunwai, and N. Yehuda. 2015. *Aggregate Cost Stickiness in GAAP Financial Statements and Future Unemployment Rate*. Working Paper, University of New South Wales, Northwestern University, University of Texas at Dallas.

Schlecker M. 2009. Credit Spreads. Einflussfaktoren, Berechnung und langfristige Gleichgewichtsmodellierung, *Dissertation*. Lohmar/Köln.

Shin, H. S. 2003. Disclosures and Asset Returns. *Econometrica* 71 (1): 105-133.

Shivakumar, L., O. Urcan, F. P. Vasvari, and L. Zhang. 2011. The debt market relevance of management earnings forecasts: evidence from before and during the credit crisis. *Review of Accounting Studies* 16 (3): 464-486.

Sironi, A. and A. Resti. 2007. *Risk Management and Shareholders' Value in Banking: from Risk Measurement Models to Capital Allocation Policies*. Chichester: John Wiley & Sons.

Sloan, R. 1996. Do stock prices fully reflect information in accruals and cash flows about future earnings? *The Accounting Review* 71 (3): 289-315.

Strube, E. 1936. Kostenremanenz und Beschäftigungsschwankungen. *Zeitschrift für Handelswissenschaftliche Forschung* 30 (10): 505-541.

Subramaniam, C. and M. L. Weidenmier. 2003. *Additional Evidence on the Sticky Behavior of Costs*. Working Paper, Texas Christian University.

Sundaram , R. K. and S. R. Das. 2016. *Derivatives: Principles and Practice. 2nd edition.* New York: McGraw-Hill Education.

Tang, D. Y. and H. Yan. 2007. *Liquidity and Credit Default Swap Spreads.* Working Paper, University of Hong Kong, Shanghai Jiao Tong University.

Tang, D. Y. and H. Yan. 2010. Market conditions, default risk and credit spreads. *Journal of Banking & Finance* 34 (4): 743-753.

Uy, A. O. O. 2011. Modeling Cost Behavior: Linear Models for Cost Stickiness. *Academy of Accounting and Financial Studies Journal* 15 (1): 25-34.

Vassalou, M. and Y. Xing. 2004. Default risk in equity returns. *Journal of Finance*, 59 (2): 831-868.

Venieris, G., V. C. Naoum, and O. Vlismas. 2015. Organisation capital and sticky behaviour of selling, general and administrative expenses. *Management Accounting Research* 26: 54-82.

Wei, S. X. and C. Zhang. 2006. Why Did Individual Stocks Become More Volatile? *The Journal of Business* 79 (1): 259-292.

Weiss, D. 2010. Cost Behavior and Analysts' Earnings Forecasts. *The Accounting Review* 85 (4): 1441-1471.

Weistroffer, C. 2009. Credit Default Swaps: Heading Toward a More Stable System. *Deutsche Bank Research Current Issues*.

Wooldridge, J. M. *Introductory Econometrics: A Modern Approach. 5th edition.* South-Western: Cengage Learning.

Yawitz, J. B. 1977. An Analytical Model of Interest Rate Differentials and Different Default Recoveries. *Journal of Financial and Quantitative Analysis* 12 (3): 481-490.

Yu, F. 2005. Accounting transparency and the term structure of credit spreads. *Journal of Financial Economics* 75 (1): 53-84.

Zhang, B. Y., H. Zhou, and H. Zhu. 2009. Explaining Credit Default Swap Spreads with the Equity Volatility and Jump Risks of Individual Firms. *The Review of Financial Studies* 22 (12): 5099-5131.

Zhu, H. 2006. An Empirical Comparison of Credit Spreads between the Bond Market and the Credit Default Swap Market. *Journal of Financial Services Research* 29 (3): 211-235.

The manufacturer's authorised representative in the EU is Springer Nature Customer Service Centre GmbH, Europaplatz 3, 69115 Heidelberg, Germany. If you have any concerns regarding our products, please contact ProductSafety@springernature.com

Printed and bound by CPI Group (UK) Ltd, Croydon, CR0 4YY
25/09/2026
02222849-0013